Library of
Davidson College

SOCIAL POLICY AND CONFLICT RESOLUTION

*BOWLING GREEN STUDIES
IN APPLIED PHILOSOPHY*

Volume VI - 1984

SOCIAL POLICY AND CONFLICT RESOLUTION

BOWLING GREEN STUDIES IN APPLIED PHILOSOPHY
Volume VI - 1984

Edited by the Faculty of the Department of Philosophy
Bowling Green State University

Thomas W. Attig
Michael Bradie
Donald Callen
James Child
Ramona T. Cormier
Douglas D. Daye
Marilyn Friedman
Robert Goodwin
Louis I. Katzner
Richard Lineback
Loy Littlefield
Fred D. Miller, Jr.
Jeffrey Paul
Michael H. Robins
Donald W. Scherer
James D. Stuart

PRINCIPAL EDITORS

Thomas Attig, Donald Callen
and R.G. Frey

The Applied Philosophy Program
Bowling Green State University
Bowling Green, Ohio

Copyright © 1984 by   The Department of Philosophy
                       Bowling Green State University

ALL RIGHTS RESERVED

Published by   The Applied Philosophy Program
                Bowling Green State University
                Bowling Green, Ohio 43403

ISBN 0-935756-07-8

CONTENTS

Preface v

Conflict Resolution and Values Pluralism

R.G. Frey, CONFLICT AND RESOLUTION: ON VALUES ANDTRADE-OFFS 1

Donald Scherer, SOME SIMPLE RATIONAL CONFLICT RESOLUTION: PROCEDURES FOR INCOMMENSURABLE VALUES 17

Justice and Scarcity

Henry West, THE CONCEPT OF JUSTICE AND CONFLICT RESOLUTION 27

George Stein, SOCIAL PHILOSOPHY, NATIONAL SOCIALISM, AND THE SCARCITY SOCIETY 38

William Aiken, USING FOOD AS A WEAPON 49

National Economic Priorities

James P. Sterba, NATIONAL DEFENSE VS. SOCIAL WELFARE 59

Edmund Byrne, DISPLACED WORKERS: WHOSE RESPONSIBILITY? 74

Jan Narveson, FULL EMPLOYMENT: THE SUPREME ECONOMIC PRIORITY 88

Strategies for Conflict Resolution

Onora O'Neill, HOW CAN WE INDIVIDUATE MORAL PROBLEMS? 104

Bill Puka, THE SAVINGS APPROACH TO SOCIAL CONFLICT 120

Tom Regan, HONEY DRIBBLES DOWN YOUR FUR: REMARKS ON ENVIRONMENTAL ETHICS 138

The Professions: Regulations and Guidelines

Maura O'Brien, THE EVOLVING ANTITRUST REGULATION OF THE PROFESSIONS 156

John Snapper, LIMITS ON THE STANDARDS OF PRIVATE ASSOCIATIONS 168

Robert Strikwerda, ON WHAT OUGHT WE VOTE? ON PROFESSIONAL ORGANIZATIONS AND PUBLIC AFFAIRS 182

PREFACE

This is the sixth volume in a series of studies in applied philosophy undertaken in order to bring traditional philosophical disciplines such as metaphysics, epistemology and ethics to bear on the illumination and resolution of social problems.

Applied philosophy is not a recent innovation. Its practical objective is prefigured by Aristotle in the Nicomachean Ethics when he says: "We are inquiring not in order to know what virtue is, but to become good." Theoretical inquiry has an important place in the total enterprise of philosophy, but the ultimate concern of applied philosophy is for the integration of theory and practice.

The papers in this volume were originally presented at a conference on Social Policy and Conflict Resolution, held at Bowling Green State University on May 4 and 5, 1984. This sixth annual conference was conducted under the auspices of the Applied Philosophy Program at Bowling Green State University and supported by a grant from the Ohio Program in the Humanities.

Members of a pluralistic society are confronted by a variety of competing ends the legitimacy of which they must assess and to which they assign varying weights. These competing ends result in conflicts between such values as national security, health, public safety, aid to the poor, education and employment opportunity, free market functioning, environmental integrity, free expression and maintenance of community standards. There are likely to be conflicts about which ends are legitimate, what weights should be assigned to them and what resources should be devoted to them. For example, how should we decide what percentage of our resources to devote to defense versus aid to the poor? The goal of this conference was to examine ways in which philosophy can contribute to the alleviation and resolution of such conflicts.

The keynote paper, by R. G. Frey, argues that in practice, when it comes down to resolving many important social conflicts, we regard competing values as commensurable; that is, "we actually do make trade-offs between values," employing an appeal to benefit, often to considerations of the harm that may be inflicted or tolerated in order to produce an overall benefit. In his comments, Donald Scherer argues that at least some values, for example life and money, are incommensurable, but that nevertheless there remain means for resolving disputes concerning such values.

The remaining papers are of four sorts: those dealing with issues of justice and scarcity, those examining national economic priorities, papers inquiring into strategies for conflict resolution, and those looking at regulations and guidelines for the professions.

In the section on justice and scarcity, Henry West examines the way utilitarian moral theory supports differing notions of justice. He argues that we appeal to justice in situations of conflict principally in order to place moral constraints on resolution by force. George Stein makes a case for the view that insofar as social philosophy has failed to develop rational and humane ways of resolving social conflicts that recognize the problem of a global scarcity of resources, the door is left open for National Socialist-like maneuvers by communities seeking their own survival, if need be at the expense of others. William Aiken argues that it is generally unwise to use food as a weapon in order to destabilize a government, the consequences of such an effort being highly unpredictable.

In the section on national economic priorities, James Sterba claims that a legitimate national defense policy will seek an optimal military security defined in terms of maintaining something less than weapons systems that are superior in destructive capability (or even equal in destructive capacity) to those of one's adversary. Yet he stresses that social welfare is obligatory and that in normal circumstances both the needs of the poor and an optimal military security should be satisfied. Edmund Byrne looks at the conflicting claims concerning the responsibilities and rights of labor and management in dealing with the displacement of workers by technological development. Jan Narveson argues that disputes about national priorities should not be settled by political processes. Rather, in the interests of liberty and simple efficiency, economic decisions should be left to individuals, it being difficult to see how, from a moral point of view, we will be any the worse for that.

In the section on strategies for conflict resolution, Onora O'Neill examines a number of ways in which one might attempt to individuate the moral problems which need resolving, the problem being that it is difficult if not impossible to escape the consequence that differing moral theories pick out different problems as being morally significant. Bill Puka considers the same theme and uses the example of forming an urban policy to show that an overriding concern should be given to "saving" as many as possible of the divergent values that are engaged within particular policy disputes. Tom Regan argues that on the plausible assumption that an anthropocentric ethics is inadequate, we should look to the concept of inherent value as a way of extending our moral sentiments to some non-human species.

In the final section, which deals with regulations and guidelines for the professions, Maura O'Brien offers a critique of the Supreme Court's reasoning on the restraint of antitrust activity, claiming that the Court has no means for weighing ethical concerns against the concern for maximizing economic efficiency. Its "rule of reason" restraint fails to encompass cases where anticompetitive actions, while not enhancing competition in the long run, do create a public benefit. John Snapper argues that the courts ought to have jurisdiction over the rules of private associations extending beyond antitrust statutes, even to such trivial matters as the level of dues. Robert Strikwerda examines the question of how to determine the issues which are appropriate for formal consideration by a voluntary professional association as such. He defines several criteria for identifying those issues which are appropriately considered.

We wish to thank Patricia Bressler and Tamara Sharp for their efforts in making the conference a success and for their tireless assistance in the preparation of this manuscript.

SOCIAL CONFLICT AND RESOLUTION:
ON VALUES AND TRADE-OFFS

R. G. Frey

All too often, as particular social conflicts are examined and their proposed resolutions critically assessed, an issue of very general importance is overlooked.[1] This is the question of whether, to the extent that social conflicts take the form of conflicts of values, all values may be compared with and weighed against each other. If they can, then we might initially believe that all social conflicts, as conflicts of values, can be rationally resolved; the preferred resolution will be the one in which, as a result of the comparison, the more weighty of the values in the circumstances overrides the other. If, however, all values cannot be compared with and weighed against each other, then we might initially doubt that all social conflicts are capable of being rationally resolved; for if we cannot compare the two values and weigh them against each other, then we seem deprived of any reason per se for preferring one resolution of the conflict to another.

These two views of value conflicts, on one of which values are commensurable, i.e., can be compared with and weighed against each other, on the other of which they are incommensurable, matter enormously to the areas of social and public policy (as well as to private morality). The reason is obvious: we inhabit a world in which people come into conflict, often at the deepest level of values; social harmony, therefore, seems to dictate that these conflicts be resolved. But if they cannot be rationally resolved (we are not here concerned with the use of coercion), social harmony may well be in jeopardy.

Three observations must be added. First, those who hold the incommensurability thesis need not hold it with respect to all values. They may allow that some, even a great many, values are commensurable and that conflicts between commensurable values are resolvable. One value can be traded off against the other, and an increase in the one value can compensate for (a non-increase or) a decrease in the other. It is with cases involving incommensurable values that a question arises of how they are to be resolved. Second, those who hold the commensurability thesis are not committed to the view that, because the comparison of values is possible, the resolution of social conflicts is a direct, simple, easy task. Plainly, matters are more complicated than this. Third, and most importantly, it must not be assumed that adherents to the two theses hold different things to be valuable. Of course, all of us will probably think some things valuable that our friends do not; nevertheless, for most of us, there is a considerable overlap in values, and this can and typically will be true of adherents to the two theses. Thus, both may and typically will value human dignity; the issue between them is whether dignity is a commensurable or incommensurable value. Can it be compared with other values and outweighed by them? Can it, that is, be traded off against some other value or values?

That we make trade-offs in public life, and that we often have to make them, is undoubtedly the case, and this is why it is difficult to convince people that we cannot compare values. Retreat into some thesis of the incommensurability of values appears per se at odds with the actual trade-offs we make in communal life.

Indeed, for a large range of that life, trade-offs are of its very essence. Below, I focus upon a type of trade-off of this sort and then link it to the issue of the allocation of resources.

I

As a community, we sometimes harm one person or group in order to benefit another person or group. Conscription is a case in point, as is the operation of the tax system; thus, single people without children pay taxes for which they receive no direct benefit, as in free lunch programs for the children of the poor and in the operation of the public schools. (One might claim that the enrichment of the general public through the education of children was a benefit to single people; but this is a benefit that (i) married people with children also in part enjoy through a forced subsidy from single people and (ii) single people cannot voluntarily accept or reject. They are compelled to support the children of others, as they would not be if only users of the public schools were taxed, in spite of the fact that they have no voice in the decisions of others to have children.[2])

The terms 'harm' and 'benefit' are not to be understood morally; they simply stand for loss and gain, disadvantage and advantage, pain and pleasure, frustration and satisfaction of desires, or whatever. In the case of conscription, for example, the conscriptee's interests are harmed--he cannot now pursue what he wants to pursue--in order to foster the interests of others in a secure defense; but there is as yet no moral significance imputed to the losses and gains involved. Talk of 'harm' and 'benefit' is just another way of talking about the fact that the conscriptee has suffered a loss in freedom and that others have enjoyed a gain in security.

Importantly, we treat the benefit as compensation for the harm. We treat the gain in security enjoyed by the community as compensation for the conscriptee's loss in freedom; we treat that gain that married people and their children receive through free public education as compensation for the loss that single persons undergo in having to part with a larger share of their incomes. In the absence of the off-setting gain, we would not demand that the conscriptee suffer the loss he does; the gain to others, we think, justifies the loss to him. Cases of the sort I am discussing, therefore, are unlike the usual cases of compensation in, say, tort law, where a subsequent gain, in the form of restitution, accrues to the person or group that incurred the initial loss; in the free lunch program, the gain accrues to the poor while the loss is incurred by others.

Obviously, the 'we' I am speaking of here is the community, viewed collectively, as if it were a person. Whether through its elected councils or officials, the community makes decisions for the conduct of social life; it decides what policies will govern that life. Since the community is nothing more than the individual members who comprise it, viewed collectively, the need to make communal decisions is the need of these individuals to govern themselves in their interactions with each other.

In social and public life, then, we make trade-offs of the sort I have described, and we make them regularly. Any view that says we do not or cannot make them, any view that deprives us of the conditions for making them would seem doubtful.

II

In communal life, we often have to make trade-offs. Thus, if a community can only hire a few outstanding teachers if it fires several firemen, and if it decides to hire the teachers, then it trades off a degree of safety for a boost to education and treats the gains in one as compensation for the losses in the other. If, financially, the community cannot both hire the teachers and retain the firemen, then it must decide which it wants more and so which value to fund. Since communities do in fact make these decisions, it is hard to see how safety and education can be values that cannot be compared and weighed against each other. So let us consider a case involving life, which, if any value is thought incommensurable, it will probably be.

Suppose a community that does not have limitless funds finds itself at the end of the fiscal year with a reasonable sum of money in hand, to do with as it sees fit, and suppose further that two camps have formed as to how the money should be spent: one favors buying additional kidney dialysis machines for the local hospital, where there are not enough to meet present demand, whereas the other favors repairing the community's highly travelled streets, which are in an atrocious state. Both projects are admirable, and if there were enough money, the community would certainly want to fund both; but funds are tight, and the local citizenry oppose further tax increases. How, then, should the available money be spent? Do we trade off buying the machines for paving the streets? Or do we go the other way?

In social and public life, the decisions we face between competing values, such as this one, can be seen as decisions about social priorities. Such decisions in fact often amount to allocation problems, and answers to such problems in the public arena must typically be framed in the light of scarce resources.[3] Thus, we can pave the streets only if we do not buy the machines; we can hire a few teachers only if we fire a few firemen; and so on. Decisions about trade-offs seem inescapable, seen in this light.

Importantly, the sorts of things people often say about such cases as these are not on the whole very helpful. To decide the case on grounds of importance runs up against the facts (i) both life (for this in the end is what the machines are about) and paving the streets are important to the community, and, indeed, perhaps equally so, (ii) a ranking of values in terms of importance seems already to presuppose some decisions about social priorities, and (iii) some scale for determining and measuring importance has not been given us. To decide the case on grounds of need runs up against the same three facts as importance. To announce that the case is too difficult and so for the community to wash its hands of it is (i) to fail to secure, wholly or partially, either of the two conflicting values, (ii) to abdicate responsibility for the tough decisions required of us by social life, and (iii) to fail to come to grips with the problem of disagreement in ends and values among members of society. To opt for taxing citizens still further, even to the extent of taking the bulk of their incomes, runs up against the facts that (i) they may not vote such increases, (ii) coercion may, therefore, be required to extract further money from them, (iii) coercion may breed physical and other forms of violence in return, and (iv) it is exceedingly improbable, because such clashes as the one described are so numerous and because the values competing in them so varied and extensive, that even this solution will suffice to guarantee that all of our values will be funded to the degree we should like. Finally, always to opt for a compromise--in this case, to buy a few machines and to pave a few streets--is itself to make assumptions about comparing values and trade-offs and to accept the paving of some streets as compensation for not securing all the machines the money might have bought.

That we make trade-offs does not make it any less necessary to say how we make them, that is, to provide their rationale. I remain some form of utilitarian,[4] and I would hope that a sufficiently rich utilitarianism, construed as a theory of trade-offs between values, could serve to provide this rationale. It is obvious how I should begin: if we ask community members to vote their preferences, ranking these according to how strongly members prefer the different options on offer; if the scale for measuring strength of preference and so for ranking preferences is ordinal, involving judgments of more or less, rather than cardinal; then we might at least start off by seeing whether we could maximize most people's most powerful preferences.[5] But I shall not explore and try to develop this theory of trade-offs, since utilitarianism is not my concern in this paper; rather, I want to retain the focus upon the commensurability and incommensurability theses.

III

In trying to decide between buying the machines and paving the streets, the trade-off view compares the value of having the machines with the values of better streets. But how exactly do we compare lives with paved streets? The problem is not unlike one we have all faced when we have been asked to say who was the better novelist, Melville or Joyce, without having been provided with the measure of comparison that enables us to compare them. To call saving lives and better streets commensurable values is to imply that they can be measured by the same standard (all we need to decide is whether saving lives or better streets is more valuable in the circumstances, and the claim that one thing is more valuable than another--we do not require a cardinal scale of measurement--rests upon a measure that enables us to determine more or less). But what is that single measure on which the two values can be weighed against each other? Without that scale, the values cannot be compared; without comparison, they cannot be traded off against each other. Plainly, the scale has to be supplied.

Suppose first, however, the adherent to the incommensurability thesis inserts himself into the picture: the value of lives cannot be compared with the value of better streets, because there is no single scale of comparability and measurement on which they can both be plotted and weighed against each other. How, then, can we decide the case before us? Yet, we actually do make decisions such as this one and so decide upon the order of social priorities for the allocation of resources. Of course, one might say that, in such cases, we just have to intuit what the decision should be; but there are all kinds of problems with this solution, not the least of which is that people's intuitions differ. And the same can be said of a solution that relies upon private, idiosyncratic judgment.

It is important not to make a serious mistake: an adherent to the incommensurability thesis claims that the values of saving lives and better streets cannot be compared because there is no single measure (more and less are quantities, which is why I speak of a measure) in terms of which the comparison can be made; he does not claim that, say, the value of saving lives always has greater weight than the value of paving the streets. To say that one thing weighs more than another implies a common scale of measurement, which is precisely what is held to be absent.

The adherent to the incommensurability thesis may want to suggest the following: to claim that values cannot be compared on a common measure is not itself to claim that values cannot be compared at all; some comparisons may be possible. Per se, however, this line of argument does not help unless the ways in which the comparisons are made help us to decide the conflict, and more needs to be said about the comparisons themselves before we can pronounce on this. Most importantly, those comparisons cannot make implicit reliance upon a common measure, which is what I think all talk of more and less does; thus, for example, those comparisons cannot take the form of reliance upon importance to or need of the community, because without some common measure in terms of which to express talk of importance or need we could not determine which of two conflicting values was more important or was more needed. A hierarchy of importance or need requires just such a measure.

The adherent to incommensurability may adopt a different line: to claim that values cannot be compared on a common measure is not itself to claim that each of the conflicting values cannot be expressed on a scale or measure. The problem here is that, if each of the conflicting values is expressed on a scale or measure, if those scales or measures are different, and if they themselves cannot each be expressed in terms of a further, common scale or measure, then the fact that each of the values can be placed on a scale or measure does not help to resolve the conflict.

A still different line would be this: to claim that values cannot be compared on a common scale or measure is not itself to claim that reasons cannot be given for preferring one side of the conflict to the other. The difficulty is that reasons can be given on both sides; to decide the conflict, we need to weigh the reasons and to come down on the weightier side.[6] But how are we to determine the weightier set of reasons, unless we are able to express both in terms of a scale or measure amenable to both?

In the end, however, probably the most important point is that we actually do trade off human life against other values, and money is very frequently the medium of exchange or comparability. For example, suppose a person is admitted to the local hospital with a life-threatening disease for which there is presently no cure: though we value saving life, we do not devote the hospital's entire yearly budget to the search for a cure with which to save the man; we do not close our parks and schools, sell off the contents of our museums and libraries, and use the money to try to save this man. Though we value saving life, we do not place either an infinite value upon it or a value so high as to preclude the use of money to secure other values. Again, we lament the cost in human life that cars and trucks bring in their wake; but we do not ban their use in order to eliminate the problem. To do that would be too costly, in terms of personal convenience, getting our goods and produce to market, the movement of the work force, and so on.

Thus, we do trade off life against other values and so do not ascribe it a 'value beyond compare'. In such cases, there is an acceptable level of death, acceptable in the sense that there is a point, difficult though it is to establish, beyond which we will not sacrifice other values to that of life. Our man admitted to the hospital is eventually asked to go, even though he wants to live and in no way consents to his death.

If it is remembered that we are talking about conflicts of values in social and public life, where the pressure for a resolution of such conflicts is paramount if (i) we are to reach decisions on priorities and to govern ourselves, (ii) we are to allocate scarce resources over competing policies and values, and (iii) we are to live in harmony even though we have different ends and values, then the search for a medium of comparability through which to make trade-offs, even involving life, is hardly surprising. Such conflicts can be seen as allocation problems, and money forms one medium of exchange or comparability. This is hardly surprising, since money forms the terms in which many allocation problems in public life present themselves; and we do in resolving such problems allocate money over competing ends and values. In asking how much we are prepared to spend to save a life at the expense of some other value, such as better streets, we attempt to bring to a focus our comparison of the different values.

IV

It may seem that, in goods in which there is a market, money may be able to form a medium of comparability; but we are concerned here with social and public policy generally and, hence, also with goods or values in which there is presently no market. One may be considerably more hesitant about the use of money as a medium of comparability here because one may feel that there are values for which money is simply an inappropriate measure.

In reply, five general observations might be made. First, with goods in which there is no actual market, we are being asked to envisage a hypothetical market and, in the context of that market, to find a market value for these goods. The mere fact that there is no actual market in some good does not prevent our envisaging a hypothetical market in which that good acquires a market value. Thus, though there is no actual market in the value of human life, we can nevertheless raise the question, in connection with my earlier example, of how much we would be willing to spend to save a man's life, if he were in the condition I described and if other values were threatened, should expenditure in his case steadily mount. We can ask similar questions in the clash between education and safety and in the case of other conflicting values.

Second, for most of us, to think of values in terms of money is both slightly distasteful, since we tend not to approve of a too close concern with money, and somewhat embarrassing, since we might be taken to think as a result that money is the only thing ultimately of value.[7] But to agree to use money as a measure of how valuable something is to one is not to endorse the view that only money matters or that one can be bought or that only a life of luxury is worth living. Money is being used as a yardstick for measuring value, not as the only value or as a demon god telling one what to value.

Third, we are discussing conflicts of values in social and public life, where many of these in fact amount to allocation problems: we have to decide among a great many projects and programs, which reflect different ends and values, which to fund. We cannot wash our hands of these decisions because we should then typically fail either to secure or to secure to an adequate degree any of the competing values; but if we address these decisions, we do so from the start in part in a financial context. Decisions on social priorities and, therefore, on the formation of a (changeable) hierarchy of priorities are never far removed from financial considerations, since part of the reason we are trying to reach such decisions and to form such hierarchies in the first place is, to repeat, in order to allocate financial resources over competing projects and programs that reflect different ends and values. It is especially important not to overlook the fact, therefore, that many conflicts of values in public life already present themselves to us in financial form. For example, enormous numbers of people make their living from growing tobacco, and we help to protect them from the vagaries of the market through federal price supports; but we also spend large sums of money on cancer research, myriad health programs to combat problems caused by smoking, and attempts to discourage people from taking up the noxious weed. Though this state of affairs may be unusual and doubtless will in time have to be changed, it represents an attempt by us in the short term to reach some kind of trade-off between the competing values of livelihood and health.

Fourth, with elusive values such as life, it is tempting to think that they cannot be measured by money. One of the major reasons some people think this is that they focus exclusively and in the abstract on the question of how to place a monetary figure on a life; they ignore trying to become clear about, e.g., what we are not prepared to do or to see happen, in order to save a life. To recall my earlier example, most of us are not prepared, in order to save the man in question, to liquidate our libraries and museums or even to go very far in the direction of spending a portion of the hospital's yearly budget. There is a sum of money we will not spend to save this man, even though we concede saving a life to be valuable; and although it may be difficult to decide just what this sum is and difficult, therefore, to decide just when we cease our efforts to save the man, we will cease those efforts.

It may be thought that I would change my tune if, instead of the social or public domain, we were concerned with my private affairs and if the life to be saved were that of my child; but I am not clear that I would. One of the most difficult decisions a friend of mine has had to make is how to divide up his resources between his mentally handicapped child on the one hand and his two normal children on the other. He naturally attempts to compensate his handicapped child by diverting more of his resources in that child's direction; but he is also firmly of the opinion that there is a limit beyond which he cannot go in that direction, at the expense of his other children. For example, he will not use money he saves monthly for the normal children's education in order to enable the handicapped child to receive enhanced treatment at a clinic in Europe. There is, in other words, a sum of money he will not spend on a handicapped life at the expense of normal lives, and judgments of this sort, though unpalatable to have to make, are not at all rare in our private affairs.

Or consider something even so elusive as human dignity:[8] how can money measure it? Yet, consider: a great many prisons and detention centers in this country are seriously overcrowded and do very little to protect inmates' privacy. With vastly more money, we could alter existing buildings and facilities and construct new ones that saw to this protection. But would you forego all public funding of the arts to secure this value? If the answer is yes, then we can up the ante; if the answer is no, then you seem reduced to trade-offs, to trading off (so much money for) privacy and dignity for (so much money for) opera.

Fifth, money is being suggested as an initial medium of comparability of values, not the only or necessarily the final such medium. For it is the medium in which allocation problems, which involve as solutions the allocation of resources over competing ends and values, typically present themselves to us, and it represents an attempt to get away from reliance upon decision-makers' intuitions or private judgments in the search for such solutions.

Were I concerned in this paper with utilitarianism, I should go on to sketch my conception of it as a theory of trade-offs, with a value theory and account of utility framed around preferences or desires and their satisfaction and with the use of hypothetical markets wherein money is the initial, though not the only or necessarily the final measure of strength of preference or desire. Since a simple utilitarianism will no longer do, my sketch would consume many pages. Here, I want only to stress that utilitarianism is something over and above the commensurability thesis.

Construed as a theory of trade-offs, utilitarianism is inimical to the claim that there are incommensurable values. But that is not what is peculiarly utilitarian about the theory; what makes the theory utilitarian is not its acceptance of the view that values can be expressed upon a single scale of desire-satisfaction but rather its commitment to summing or aggregating desire satisfactions across persons. Utilitarianism is a maximizing theory, concerned with the maximization of desire-satisfaction; it focuses upon the total amount of desire-satisfaction, which is determined by summing or aggregating desire-satisfactions across persons. I do not see why someone who thinks that values are commensurable, however, need be committed to a maximizing theory. I think he is very likely to embrace such a theory, because I think the attractions of utilitarianism, to someone who accepts that values are commensurable, will be powerful; but I can see no necessity in the matter. Thus, though an utilitarian is committed to the commensurability thesis, an adherent to that thesis need not be committed to utilitarianism.

V

In harming one person or group in order to benefit another, we treat the benefit as compensation for the harm. When we think morally about such cases and so about whether what was (or is to be) done was (or is) right, we regard the benefit as justifying the infliction or toleration of the harm. This appeal to benefit is widely employed and in diverse contexts, which are by no means confined to cases involving harms and benefits only to humans, as with conscription, free school lunches, and the public schools; thus, the appeal is widely employed today in order to justify painful experiments upon animals for the benefit of humans.

The appeal to benefit is an integral part of problems to do with the allocation of scarce resources. Were a resource infinite in quantity, it could satisfy an infinite number of demands upon it; but a finite resource requires us to exercise discrimination over which demands to satisfy. Thus, the teachers can be hired only if the firemen are fired, the dialysis machines can be purchased only if the streets are not repaired, and so on. Gains and losses are both direct and indirect. On the plus side, in addition to the direct gains to the teachers hired, there are the indirect gains to students and, through them, hopefully, to the rest of us; on the minus side, in addition to the direct losses to the firemen, there are the indirect losses to their families and, as well, to the rest of us through diminished safety arrangements.

Now the justification we give for firing the firemen invokes the appeal to benefit, and it is hard to see how we could either explain or justify our decision to fire them if we were forbidden to invoke it. For we do not fire these men and increase risks to public safety for no reason at all or for a reason of merely trivial concern; we do not inflict or tolerate loss so lightly. Rather, we take increased risks over safety because of the expected return in the form of enhanced education; plainly, we are allowing enhanced education to compensate for diminished safety, and this sort of thing seems of the essence to our decisions allocating scarce resources over competing values. To the extent that one employs the appeal to benefit in the search for a solution to these sorts of problems, to that extent one treats the conflicting values as commensurable. For how else could a gain in one compensate for a loss in another? The appeal justifies, and only justifies, by allowing compensation for the loss incurred; but enhanced education can only compensate for diminshed safety if, as it were, so much additional educational opportunity and prospective excellence could offset so much less fire service manpower and reduction in safety. In other words, the appeal to benefit turns upon the notion of compensation between values, which itself seems to require that values be regarded as commensurable.

I have restricted my remarks here to cases involving the appeal to benefit, precisely because there may be cases where one would repudiate compensation between values and so where the appeal would be barred. These would be cases in which one maintained that no amount of increase, however great, in some other value could compensate for any amount of decrease, however slight, in this value. There is nothing fixed here, and whether compensation is acceptable or not is itself a matter for the community and its preferences; but even a cursory inspection of social and public policy decisions we actually make in cases of conflicting values shows that we in our communities do not often repudiate compensation. The very prevalence of the appeal to benefit is evidence of this.

Suppose, however, a community maintained this: it will not accept any amount of enhanced educational opportunity and excellence as compensation for any loss in safety because safety is more valuable than education. Such a position ostensibly bars trading off firemen for teachers by appeal to benefit, since gains in one end or value cannot now, it will be said, offset and compensate losses in another end or value. But the problem here is to understand the phrase 'more valuable than'. It may be simply a way of stating the community's preferences: a majority do not now favor more money for education at the expense of safety. Obviously, however, the community's preferences need only change for education then to become more valuable than safety. It is considerably more likely, therefore, that the phrase 'more valuable than' is to be seen as a way of trying to say something about safety and education without tying them to the community's preferences; safety, it might be said, is objectively more valuable than education. The problem now, however, is the one noted earlier: one thing can only be more valuable or important or cruel or shameful or blue than another if a scale or measure is specified on which both things can be placed. Comparative judgments of more and less require a medium of comparison, and in the absence of this medium the determination of more and less cannot be made. Thus, safety can only be more valuable than education if a scale or measure of value is specified which makes this the case; but to provide this scale or measure and to place the two values upon it is to concede that the two values are commensurable. Again, one might say that safety is to be placed on one scale or measure, education on another, and each is valuable according to where it falls upon their respective scales or measures; but this sort of procedure could not tell one that safety was more valuable than education. A third scale or measure, upon which both values are placed is needed for that, which yields the result once again that the two values are commensurable. And if they are commensurable, why cannot a certain loss in safety be traded off for a certain gain in education?

In short, we actually do make trade-offs between values, do allocate scarce resources between competing values, and do employ the appeal to benefit. To the extent that we employ the appeal in those cases of inflicting or tolerating harm in order to produce benefit, which includes all our allocation problems here, we seem (at least prima facie) constrained to regard the conflicting values in these cases as commensurable. To be instructed to forego the appeal to benefit, however, is not only to be false to what we actually do in these cases but also to leave us per se without an explanation or a justification of why we inflict or tolerate the harm to the person or group in question.

Admittedly, much more needs to be said both to fill out and to justify parts of this sketch before it can be anything more than tentative; but it does indicate how one might try to adduce at least one strand of support for the view that decisions on priorities in social and public life demand that values be regarded as commensurable.

University of Liverpool

NOTES

1. It is not always overlooked. See, for example, Jonathan Glover, 'Assessing the Value of Saving Lives', in G. Vesey, (ed.), *Human Values* (Sussex, The Harvester Press, 1978); James Griffin, 'Are there incommensurable values?', *Philosophy and Public Affairs,* vol. 7, 1977, and Griffin's 'Bentham and Modern Utilitarianism', *Revue Internationale de Philosophie,* vol. 141, 1982; Bernard Williams, *Morality: An Introduction to Ethics* (Cambridge, Cambridge University Press, 1972), pp. 101 ff., and Williams' 'Conflicts of Values', in A. Ryan, (ed.), *The Idea of Freedom* (Oxford, Oxford University Press, 1979); and Thomas Nagel's 'The Fragmentation of Value', in *Mortal Questions* (Cambridge, Cambridge University Press, 1979). My paper is indebted to and draws upon these works.

2. In Britain, where a family allowance scheme is in operation, even middle-class parents are entitled to child-allowance for each of their children. In effect, a married couple with children receives a subsidy from single people, even if the couple enjoys a handsome income.

3. Any resource that exists in finite amounts can become scarce.

4. To say exactly what form would take up too much space here and divert us from the main concern of the paper.

5. For an example of such a start, see Griffin's 'Are there incommensurable values?', *op. cit.*

6. See Glover, 'Assessing the Value of Saving Lives', *op. cit.,* p. 215.

7. See Glover, 'Assessing the Value of Saving Lives', *op. cit.,* pp. 212 ff.

8. See Williams, *Morality: An Introduction to Ethics,* pp. 102 ff.

SOME SIMPLE RATIONAL CONFLICT RESOLUTION PROCEDURES FOR INCOMMENSURABLE VALUES

Donald Scherer

The heart of Professor Frey's paper is a universal claim: every value is commensurable with every other. The premises Professor Frey uses to support his claim are that (1) we do compare and weigh pairs of values against each other whenever they conflict, and (2) only such comparing and weighing allows choices between conflicting values to be rational. From these premises Frey apparently concludes that (1') we do treat every value as if it were commensurable with every other, and (2') we ought (for the sake of being rational in our conflict resolving) to treat all values as commensurable with each other.

Since Professor Frey's claim is universal, its falsification requires simply one contrary instance. The most propitious choice of such an instance would probably be what we vaguely call the value of human life. For the value of life is often claimed to be incommensurable with the value of mere commodities.[1] Indeed, Professor Frey recognizes the centrality of this value to his argument. He takes it that if any value is incommensurable, the value of life is. So, rather than actually arguing that every value is commensurable with every other, he focuses on showing how the value of life is taken to be and (for the sake of rationality) must be taken to be commensurable with (all) other values.

Now kidnappers whose ransom demands go unmet sometimes kill their abductees. So the descriptive claim that the value of life is sometimes taken to be commensurable with the value of money is non-controversial. Accordingly, I shall focus on the normative claim that rationality requires the value of life to be taken as commensurable with other values. The claim to be examined is that when the value of life conflicts with the value of some commodities, rationality requires that we resolve the dispute by comparing and weighing the values commensurably.

I do not believe that rationality requires a commensurability of the value of life. For example, we can imagine a society in which, when two parties have a conflict of values, they take it to their sage who hears their claim, reflects and, without any weighing of the values, renders a decision which the disputants are socialized to accept. Perhaps the sage relies on precedent or principles (as judges in our society often do) or discernment (like Solomon). Since the disputants accept the judgment of the sage, the conflict is resolved.[2]

In the preceding paragraph, of course, I have argued for the rationality of a procedure in terms of its outcome. If, in a given society, there is a widely respected role, and the individuals occupying that role so behave as to maintain the respect of the members of the society, then the pronouncements of the occupiers of the role may be sufficient to resolve otherwise intractable disputes. From the point of view of the fully resolved outcome, nothing could be more rational. But some philosophers may feel that the outcome can be no more acceptable than the process which produced it. And this much seems to be true: (especially) outside the judicial sphere, we live in a society in which people are not socialized to accept the resolution of conflict. Consequently, when some party does not favor a proposed outcome, the party tends to translate any dissatisfaction with the outcome into a search for a ground to complain about the process which produced it. And, accordingly, oblique processes fall into disfavor because they block this dispute-continuing procedure. (Of course, given some real conflicts, rational dispute-continuing procedures may be prudent.) Consequently we view the articulation of means of conflict resolution as a good, an evaluation which gives impetus to the development of "compare and weigh" processes of social conflict resolution.[3]

This sociology, however, should not obscure from us the logical point implicit in imagining people socialized differently from us. If it is a particular socialization and social organization which lead us to demand a transparent process of dispute resolution, then it is not rationality <u>simplicater</u> which requires that conflicts of value be resolved only through assuming the commensurability of values.

But we are who we are. And am I conceding that what I have called a transparent process of rational dispute-resolution requires that values be regarded as commensurable? No, and to defend this position I shall, in what follows, articulate in outline and defend as rational, dispute resolution procedures which compare competing values but do not weigh them as the values of commodities are regularly weighed against each other.

Before proceding, however, let me clarify the concept of (in)commensurability. A strength of utilitarianism and of cost/benefit analysis has been the appeal of objectivity to be found in a quantitative (cardinal or ordinal) scale of measurement. If values A and B are defined as commensurable only if they are compared on a common quantitative scale of measurement, then in the following, I shall certainly provide no commensurability. I shall, however, compare, e.g., life and livelihood. I shall argue that they differ with regard to objectively specifiable qualities. They are thus comparable. But this certainly says nothing about weighing on quantitative scales of measurement. Objective comparison, I shall say, grounds arguments between incommensurable values, so that conflicts can be rationally resolved without quantitative methods.

What, then, do I propose as a model for the resolution of conflicts between incommensurable values? Actually I have two suggestions. The first is simple hierarchy building. The form of the hierarchy building argument is that value A should be chosen over value B because value A is the more important value. Of course the danger of such an argument is that my judgment of importance may provide only a subjective ground of comparison. Recurring to Professor Frey's roads, for example, we may note that if I own no car, the state of the roads may seem less important to me than to you, especially if the pizza business you own makes most of its money on deliveries. Thus hierarchy building can succeed as a strategy of conflict resolution only if "important" can have a definition which reflects the common situation of the parties to the dispute. How this is possible we may see from an examination of the tobacco subsidy example.

The state of a person's health is more fundamentally valuable than the viability of the person's method of earning a living. This is so both because (1) in the course of time a person can replace one method of earning a living with another, and because (2) if one loses one's health (that is, dies of cancer) how one makes a living is moot, whereas if one loses one's job (that is, loses governmental support for the tobacco industry) the state of one's health remains important, especially given that without one's health one shall be hard pressed to find a new way of earning a living. These comparisons are objective: they depend not one whit on whether one is a tobacco grower. The value of health is, thus, objectively more fundamental than is the value of livelihood. From which premise it can be concluded that, rationally speaking, the government ought to phase out support for tobacco growing quite independently of its support for cancer research, especially since the vagaries of the market to which Professor Frey alludes owe in important part to the decline in smoking among Americans who increasingly value their health more than they value the oral gratification smoking provides.[4]

I suffer no illusion that one can always argue (as I have above) how comparatively fundamental two values are on grounds of replaceability and dependent value.[5] A conflict between the value of my life and the value of yours will not normally be resolvable through hierarchy building. (The commensurability here is between the value of two lives.) Objectively the value of each is fundamental in the same ways. As long as egalitarianism is taken seriously, hierarchy building will seem an irrelevant strategy for resolving many of the conflicts between the value of x in your case and the value of x in mine. Still a substantial point has been made here. Since objective comparisons can sometimes be made without the use of quantitative methods, it is false that without weighing the alternatives rational conflict resolution is impossible.[6]

But may it not be objected that the simple kind of hierarchy building described above can seldom be formed? Do I concede the need for Professor Frey's quantitative methods elsewhere? No, I do not, and I shall attempt to explain myself by sketching a more general non-quantitative model of decision making.

I begin with Professor Frey's observation that when a patient is dying we do not spend all our available resources attempting to save the life of the patient. We trade off the value of the dying patient's life. Why is this and how can it be, if the value of life is incommensurable? In the following paragraphs I shall give several answers to this question, since there seem to be separate sufficient justification for this practice.

1. In the first place, devoting the entire resources of humankind to the saving of the patient's life often would not save the patient. Suppose the patient's heart has stopped beating for half an hour before the patient is resuscitated. Under normal conditions, the patient will have experienced brain death. Brain cells do not regenerate themselves, and no human being has the foggiest idea of how to regenerate brain cells. In this case, then, the devoting of the resources would be a waste. Thus, abstracting, we see that the premise that there is an obligation to save human life will certainly not yield the conclusion that all resources should be utilized to (attempt to) save unsaveable human life. "'Ought'" implies "'can'" limits the obligation to save human life to those cases in which human life is (reasonably projectable as) saveable. In other words, whereas Frey glosses the cost of saving the dying patient as too high, I gloss the spending of the money as a foolish attempt to do the impossible. The maxim "Do not engage in futile action," is not an admission of the commensurability of life with other values. It suggests the entirely appropriate recognition that we do not compromise our evaluation of life by not attempting to save unsaveable lives.

2. Moreover, in our socially complex world, goals may be unachievable because, although an appropriate technology exists, the social institutions and practices required to utilize the technology are not in place and cannot be developed within a given timeframe. The inventions of a technical medical apparatus and of a surgical procedure, for example, do not imply the existence of sufficient equipment and trained surgeons to handle the patients' needs at any given time. Both the making of the equipment and the teaching of the surgeons must pre-date any obligation to save the lives of the patients. In this case, as in the previous one, 'ought' implies 'can'.[7]

Since this point is tricky, perhaps it deserves restatement. No one thinks that a human death from a tornado compromises the dignity of human life: such death is thought uncontrollable. The cases that trick us are the cases where human death is only controllable within certain thresholds or only manageable in certain cases because we do not try to manage it in others. But these latter cases are also cases in which death, in the aggregate, is uncontrollable. "'Ought' implies 'can'" surely applies in the threshold cases as much as in the tornado case.

3. The value of the dying patient's life is rationally traded off not only for reasons of technological or institutional (in)feasibility but also for egalitarian reasons. At any given time many patients are dying in hospitals, even many with the same medical conditions. Consequently it will regularly be true that any reason for developing a program for allocating public monies for such patients' conditions will be reason, in the long run, for allocating sufficient funding for whoever is afflicted by the condition. It would, that is, be irrational to develop allocation plans which left, say, Black victims of a disease untreated since the result would not treat similars similarly. Likewise, in many cases the spending of great resources in an attempt to save the life of some patients would be incompatible with spending similar resources to attempt to save the lives of other patients, patients, we may hypothesize, just as saveable as the one. For egalitarian reasons we find it irrational to allocate all human resources to the saving of one theoretically saveable patient since that allocation will cause the death of thousands of other persons to whom treatment will by hypothesis be denied.[8]

Now let us notice that although egalitarianism has often been "incorporated" into utilitarian thought, the implications of weighing costs and benefits when two patients have needs which together outweigh resources are not egalitarian. The social benefit of saving each of two patients is not at all certain to be equal (is likely to be unequal). Thus a scheme which claims that inequality of social benefit from the saving of two lives should not be a factor concerning which life is saved is a scheme which in one important way refuses a certain commensurability. If, for example, we build an institution so that we shall not have to choose between equals, our goal of equality will imply that cost efficiency will suffer. The champion of incommensurability will not shy from this result.

4. But none of these preliminary points fully expresses the idea that the value of life is incommensurable. The idea that life has incommensurable value is the idea that the following form of argument[9] is valid:

Both Policy A and Policy B are fully feasible and egalitarian.

The value of life is jeopardized by the adoption of Policy A and not by the adoption of Policy B.

Therefore Policy A is preferable to Policy B.

Now could people reason like this? Of course, provided they could understand the terms in which the argument is stated. But if they did reason like this, would they be irrational? Not in any obvious way. Then would they be making their evaluations by implicitly weighing the alternatives? Only in the (irrelevant) sense that they would be weighting the value of life as incommensurably greater than any competing value. Then what is the problem with this reasoning?

Someone might claim that the phrase "the value of life" is hopelessly vague. From this objection would follow the conclusion that even if the argument form I present is valid either it is absolutely inapplicable or (what comes to the same thing) its application is always a rationally contentious matter. For different people define their lives in different ways and come to value different things. Surely the value of life will be hopelessly variable.

To this I respond that of course variation will exist, but not hopeless variation. A structural account may show why this is true: in any human society, people are socialized not only as children but as adults, continually. An individual's socialization provides the individual with a set of expectations (1) about the range of behaviors others may initiate toward the individual, (2) about the appropriate interpretations of such behaviors and, thus, about the reasonable repertoire of responses to others' initiatives, (3) about the range of behaviors the individual can initiate with impunity and (4) about the institutions which facilitate, support, regulate or prohibit behaviors of the sorts mentioned in (1)-(3). I assume this socialization will vary in regular ways as a function of one's society, class, race, sex and age as well as idiosyncratically.

When an individual is socialized with respect to (1)-(3), the individual is taught in hundreds of concrete ways what the value of life is. Life's value (as the individual learns to understand it) is implicit in the knowledge of how one may be treated, in the knowledge of appropriate responses to such treatment and in the knowledge of what sorts of actions will not initiate sanctions or unfortunate natural consequences. Typically, the institutional structures of the society will broadly reinforce this knowledge. This broad fit will, of course, be somewhat vague, but its vagueness can hardly conceal from us the facts that different fits exist in different societies[10] and that the fit has been different at different times within the same society. So, along with some vagueness, there is real definition here.

Now it is in terms of this fit that the incommensurability of the value of life should, I believe, be defined. Consider the indefinitely many activities subsets of which might define the value of life in some society. Relative to those activities, I distinguish two possibilities: (A) within a given society the acceptability of some activities is consistently reinforced by (1)-(4), i.e., the activity squarely fits with the fit of (1)-(4), while (B) the acceptability or unacceptability of some activities is not consistently reinforced by (1)-(4).

Now difference of judgment between members of a society about the formation of social policy regarding activities falling within (B) can be rational, but the activities falling within (A) form a core of what is meant by the value of life when the value of life is said to be incommensurable. And when the value is said to be incommensurable the implication is that the safeguarding of the core of activities is (to be) hierarchically ranked over other aims of social policy. For the socialization of the members of a society creates a pattern of reasonable expectations. It is the reasonability of those expectations about what makes life worthwhile (expectations defined by the thorough congruence of the socialization which creates them) which gives them precedence over other aims of social policy.

Someone might think that my view is unhappily conservative. If men have been socialized to expectations of dominance over women in such a way that the value of their lives as men depends on that domination, am I commending the view that social policy must give priority to the meeting of this expectation? By no means. My assumption has been that of congruence among (1)-(4). The fact with respect to sexism is that socialization in our society is immensely inconsistent. This being the case, prior to the supporting of any expectations, the aim of social policy must be the achievement of a coherent practice. The basic value of egalitarianism implies that that coherence cannot rest on norms of domination. So, indeed, there is much room for reform within the scheme I present.

Why, then, do I insist on calling the value of life incommensurable? I believe my brief comments have sketched many components of an alternative rational conflict resolution strategy. The value of life, I want to say, is concretely defined by a society's patterns of socialization. That socialization and considerations of feasibility, construed in the light of further considerations of scale, thresholds and equality, define the set of institutions the society in question must rationally regard as having a value hierarchically superior to other considerations.[11] Remaining rational conflict can then be conceptualized as a result of the tendencies of the society to change and of individual members to argue that their fellows should recognize the legitimacy of previously unrecognized claims for redefining the hierarchically superior institutional necessities. (If I had any more space, I should want to discuss the structure of such argument.)

And why should one prefer my view that the value of life is incommensurable? Because, whereas cost/benefit analysts, for example, must constantly juggle their figures to make those figures produce the desired results, my account explains why hierarchical considerations of value are justified.

Professor Frey set out to establish that conflicts between two values can be rationally resolved only if the two values are commensurable. Commensurability implies not only comparison but weighing. I have focused my reply to Professor Frey on the values of life and of money. I have sketched several means for resolving conflicts concerning the value of life without resort to any weighing on a monetary scale. I have provided some reason for calling these means rational and for rebutting Frey's view that rationality requires quantitative means. It seems, then, that asserting the incommensurability of two values with each other does not imply that one must despair of rational means of conflict resolution.

Bowling Green State University

NOTES

1. An explanation of why what is called the value of life is so vaguely defined and of that to which the value is contrasted when we speak of mere commodities will be forthcoming as part of my own account of the incommensurability of the value of life (cf. infra, pp. 6-9).

2. I suppose that part of C.A. Hooker's point in "On Deep Versus Shallow Theories of Environmental Pollution" (*Environmental Philosophy*, University of Pennsylvania Press, 1983) is that the locus of decision making in what he calls culturally unitary societies reinforces the incommensurability of values as the locus of decision making in market societies does not.

3. Notice that if an individual were in conflict with herself about which course of action to follow for herself (e.g., which kind of soup to order with dinner) no one would ordinarily argue that her process of decision was irrational because it was not suitably transparent.

4. The argument presented above is a teleological argument Aristotle might have made. That such an argument is impervious to philosophical objections which misconstrue the argument as concerning necessary conditions is clearly suggested by David Wiggins' interpretation of Aristotle in his article, "Deliberation and Practical Reason" (*Essays on Aristotle's Ethics,* A.O. Rorty, ed., University of California Press, 1980).

5. But neither am I conceding that replaceability and dependence are the only objective, non-quantitative criteria on the basis of which to form a simple hierarchical argument. A legitimate use of need, for instance, is suggested in footnote 8.

6. Or would Professor Frey rejoin that my argument about life's being irreplaceable and independently valuable, in contrast to livelihood's being replaceable and only dependently valuable, is an argument which shows the greater "weight" of the value of life? In that case Frey's talk of "weight" is entirely metaphorical, completely divorced from the use of quantitative methods, involving no meaning beyond the notion of inter-subjectively valid comparison.

7. Similar to this sort of case is the present situation with respect to organ donation. New chemical developments now apparently forestall the organ rejections which previously limited the demands of "qualified" recipients. But we are not organized to harvest even a large fraction of the available healthy organs. And it is entirely possible that should the day come when we do harvest the approximately 20,000 sets of organs available annually in the United States, the demand may have risen to exceed that supply.

8. This seems to be our thinking: if two persons need the transplant of a liver and only one liver is available to be transplanted, then we think it rational to transplant the one liver (and we like to be able to say that the choice of the recipient is also rational because of that party's greater need). The one liver is available; social policy did not deliberately set out to make livers available in inadequate supply; maximal advantage was simply made of the (inadequate, "natural") supply. However, to develop a scheme of supply and allocation which would deliberately underdevelop resources for meeting a known need would be irrational, i.e., inegalitarian.

9. Not that this is the only form whose validity follows from the incommensurability of values, merely that I have only the space to discuss one.

10. Such differences are well illustrated in John Kilner's article, "Who Shall Be Saved? An African Answer," The Hastings Center Report, June, 1984.

11. The point of speaking, in my earlier discussion, of simple hierarchies now becomes clear. In a simple hierarchy a quality (e.g., dependence) is analytically isolated as a basis of hierarchical ranking. In my later discussion the hierarchies are formed by explicating kinds of indicators of what the values of life involves, then ranking proposed policies by reference to the presence or absence of those indications, a much more complex hierarchical task.

THE CONCEPT OF JUSTICE AND CONFLICT RESOLUTION

Henry R. West

One role for social philosophy in regard to conflict resolution is to apply a moral appraisal to a conflict or type of conflict and to proposed resolutions. This appraisal is usually expressed in terms of justice: In what respects does each side have justice in its favor, and in what respects is a resolution of the conflict a just one. But there are conflicting conceptions of justice, and the resolution of the conflicting conceptions of justice requires the perspective of a more general moral theory to assess the relative merits of alternative conceptions.

In this essay I shall explore the application of a utilitarian moral theory to the resolution of conflicts by analyzing some ways in which utilitarianism might support several differing conceptions of justice. My principal claim is that the most important role of the appeal to justice in situations of conflict is to place moral constraints upon resolution by sheer force. The most important function, then, is to benefit the weaker party to the dispute, either through prohibiting the violation of certain basic human rights or through recognition of principles of distributive justice which promote the welfare of the least advantaged. I recognize, however, that appeals to justice on other grounds, such as desert for past action or property rights, which protect the interests of more advantaged parties, may also be useful in the peaceful negotiation of conflicts, avoiding situations where both parties lose through the resort to violence. This is a rather vague set of conclusions; I confess that I think that the chief value of this paper is in exploration rather than definite answers to problems regarding justice.

I.

I turn first to a discussion of the possible role of <u>any</u> moral position in the resolution of conflicts. By giving examples of conflicts, I want to distinguish between the role of moral considerations and the role of other elements in the resolution of conflicts. Then I I shall turn to the dictates of utilitarianism for principles of justice in conflict resolution.

"Conflict" is a word in ordinary usage; so we may think that we know what it means without a philosopher analyzing it for us, and we do. But there are various kinds of conflicts with importantly different features. One clear case is a military conflict between two nations at war or between two parties in a civil war. On the other extreme, we talk of the conflict of ideas between two philosophies or ideologies. This latter case is beyond the scope of our present discussion. But still within it, although not an armed conflict, is the conflict of <u>interests</u>, or perceived interests, between two or more parties, such as in labor-management disputes; civil court cases for the adjudication of property rights or compensation for injury; economic competition for scarce resources; or rights and freedoms where the exercise of a right or freedom by one party, such as freedom to engage in defamatory speech, is contrary to the right or freedom of another, in this example the right not to be defamed.

I want to make three general comments about conflicts and their resolution to introduce the role of moral considerations in the resolution of conflicts.

First, we can distinguish between conflicts which reflect genuine interests and those that don't, and we can distinguish the interests of some elements within a conflict from the overall interests of that side. Analysis of this has to be done case by case, but some examples will make the point. What genuine interests did Britain and Argentina have in the conflict over the Falkland Islands? There may be false values, such as national prestige, which cannot be resolved into the happiness of the individuals of a nation. Frequently what is called the "national interest" is not the interest of the nation's population. Furthermore, in analyzing whose interest within a given nation might be furthered by a policy, we may have to distinguish different groups. The Argentine junta, having engaged in a military buildup and rhetoric on the Argentine right to the islands, may have gotten itself into a position such that its interest lay in a successful invasion; but even a successful invasion would not have been in the interests of most Argentines, staggering under the debt incurred in the military buildup. Ironically, the <u>unsuccessful</u> invasion may have turned out to have been in their long-term best interests, since it resulted in the loss of power of the ruling junta; but this was not foreseeable.

A second general point is that conflicts may be based upon false assumptions about the consequences of actions. An example might be a labor-management dispute in which management believes that holding down wages will result in higher profits, but the consequences of successfully doing so will be that the best-qualified employees leave for other jobs, those that remain do even poorer work as a result of low morale, and profits suffer. An example going the other way would be where workers believe that a higher wage settlement would be in their interest when it would actually result in the company's costs of production becoming too high for the price of its product to be competitive, with the result that the company goes out of business and the workers lose their jobs altogther. These are the obvious possibilities.

A third general point that I want to make is about what counts as the "resolution" of conflicts. Some conflicts, especially military ones, can get "resolved" by annihilation of one opposing party and thus annihilation of conflict. Or the conflict can get repressed, and thus apparently resolved, by one party giving up any hope and accepting the dictates of the stronger party. From these examples it follows that resolution of a conflict is not always constrained by moral considerations. A conflict may be "settled" by brute force, whether the force of military and police power or the coercion of a political and legal system which is often equally brutal. In other cases "resolution" is again unreasonable, due to false beliefs of one or more parties. What is a genuine conflict of interests may be pacified by one party falsely believing that it is well off in its place and no longer continuing the struggle for change--or never initiating it in the first place. In other cases, resolution is achieved by bargaining, by recognition that there is a solution such that both parties can benefit without frustrating the interests of either. It may be possible for two warring parties to reach an agreement by which they exchange pieces of territory which the present possessor does not want and the future possessor does, to their mutual advantage. Exchange of prisoners is usually like that. In a labor-management dispute, it may be possible for workers to get some things that they most want, such as more control over the conditions of the workplace, which do not result in any loss of profits for employers. Thus changes may resolve conflicts to the benefit of both without any loss. Everyone may be made better off with no one being made worse off. If this is possible, there may be grounds for conflict resolution simply by recognizing this possibility.

I make these general observations in order to introduce the role of moral considerations in the resolution of conflicts. Conflicts and their resolution can be criticized, and it is the task of social philosophy to provide a basis for criticism. What can be the grounds of criticism? As some of the above examples indicate, criticism can sometimes be made on grounds of factual error; e.g., it is falsely believed that a policy will have certain results when it won't. For example, it is claimed that a progressive tax policy will benefit the poor in a capitalistic economy when it actually retards investment and economic growth while at the same time fueling inflation. Or, on the other hand, it is claimed that a regressive tax policy will benefit the poor by stimulating investment, economic modernization, increase in productivity and ultimately providing higher real wages, when it really results in a slump in consumer demand, economic recession, unemployment, and greater capital mobility to still lower wage areas of the world. This, as you recognize, is the issue between supply-siders and demand-siders in economic policy. In reality, the "facts" are not "hard" facts, and ideological viewpoints color the collection and interpretation of data to support one policy against another. This ideological bias may be a commitment to an economic theory in the narrow sense of "economic," such as Keynesian vs. anti-Keynesian theory of business cycles, or it may be a commitment to a more general social philosophy, such as general opposition to or support for state interference in the economy for purposes of social welfare, or it may be self-deception based on class bias. This example is intended to show that any line of demarcation between criticisms on the basis of moral theory is not a simple matter. But there still is a polarity between criticism on the basis of misjudgment of the consequences of a policy and criticism on the basis of values and morals. Even if there were not controversy about means-ends relationships, there might still be controversy about what ends are to be given what weight of consideration and whether all means are appropriate means for consideration. These controversies are often debated in terms of the justice of a social policy: in cases of conflicts of interests, what is a just resolution?

II

In this paper, as I have indicated, I am exploring what would be the just resolution of conflicts from the critical perspective of utilitarianism. For those who don't share the utilitarian point of view, this may seem a waste of time, just as a Darwinian might think that it is a waste of time to hear a creationist try to account for the apparent age of the earth. And it works both ways: to a utilitarian it may seem a waste of time to try to work out a theory of natural rights-- assuming that there are natural rights is like assuming creation.[1] The situation in moral philosophy is like Thomas Kuhn's characterization of science before there is a shared "paradigm" with a set of shared assumptions generating problems for further articulation and specification under new and more stringent conditions.[2] Before this, there are competing paradigms, each of which operates with a different conceptual framework and each of which has different problems to solve in making its theory intellectually satisfactory. So utilitarianism has some problems which do not exist for other theories or which are not so acute, and vice versa. For example, it is a problem for utilitarians to find some commensurability between the welfare or suffering of one person and another so that a policy can be judged as maximizing interpersonal welfare or minimizing interpersonal suffering. For a theorist whose fundamental moral category is the display of personal virtue in socially prescribed roles[3] or whose fundamental category is the adjudication of entitlement claims based on natural rights, this may not be an important issue. But such a problem, which is "internal" to utilitarianism since it is not a problem for other theories, is also in relation to other theories. It is a ground on which utilitarianism is often rejected by others, usually in two sentences. So whether utilitarianism has a theory of justice applicable to the resolution of conflicts is relevant to other theories in that they may claim to reject utilitarianism on grounds of this deficiency. They may reject utilitarianism for its inability to provide a social policy with a plausible theory of justice.

When moral considerations are invoked in the resolution of conflicts, it is usually, as I have already indicated, in the language of justice. One party claims that justice is on its side; or the other claims that justice is on its side; or a mediator seeks to get recognition of the claims of each. Utilitarianism is often criticized as having no theory of justice or as having an inadequate one, being merely an "aggregative" theory advocating maximization of welfare without any "distributive" principles for just apportionment.[4] What I want to explore here is that although justice is a concept which is different from justification on utilitarian grounds,[5] the principles of justice which would be supported by utilitarianism turn out to be very similar to those supported by some non-utilitarian theorists. In particular, some of the features of John Rawls' theory of justice would appear in utilitarian principles of justice, especially when justice is a principle of conflict resolution.

The first step in my argument is to call attention back to the role which moral considerations play in the resolution of conflicts, and here I want to make two points. The first is that moral considerations are appeals to moral reasons or sentiments in contrast to resolutions by sheer power, whether military, political, legal, or economic, and also in contrast to bargaining merely from positions of strength. In the absence of appeal to moral justice, conflicts may reach a negotiated settlement in which all parties gain something, but they may end by annihilation, or suppression, or drag on until given up. So moral claims supplement and constrain the use of force in conflicts. The second point I want to call attention to is that not all claims to justice are to be accepted as justified. One may claim to have justice on one's side without having it. Justice is a normative concept and it is the place of a moral theory to criticize from its perspective what is claimed to be justice or even what is regarded as justice in a given society. In what follows I want to keep in mind both of these points: appeals to justice function in actual social situations to constrain settlement by sheer force, but the concept of justice is subject to critical appraisal from the perspective of moral theory. With these points in mind, I think that the following observations are relevant.

When justice is invoked in the resolution of conflicts, it may function in three importantly different ways. It may be a claim by a stronger party to the legitimacy of its superior position. For example, the slave owner may cite property rights as grounds for the justice of the system of slavery. On the other hand, justice may be appealed to by or on behalf of the weaker party as a ground for greater equality of treatment or condition. Or, third, it may be invoked by a mediator or someone else on behalf of a negotiated settlement, seeking to show that each side will receive what it deserves. I want to recognize all of these as sometimes socially efficacious. Oppressed groups may come to accept their place as a matter of justice; or they may fail to win support from third parties because of the belief by those third parties that the oppressors have a right to their superior position. This occurs as well as the other two cases, where justice serves primarily as a constraint upon the exercise of brute power. But in the first case, the appeal to justice is to add legitimacy to a domination which has already been achieved by military, legal, or political force. The stronger party is in control and dictates terms, whether or not the terms are just, and the appeal to justice is largely to counter the appeal to justice made by the weaker party. In the second case, in which appeal to justice is made by the weaker party, its claim is going against domination by superior non-moral force. In this instance, if it is effective, it helps those who are otherwise less advantaged in their conflict against those who are otherwise more advantaged. I postpone for a moment the consideration of justice in mediation while discussing these two contrasting cases.

Suppose that there were never any efficacy in appeals to justice in either of these two cases. This would suit well the stronger party, for it would dominate with its non-moral strength. This would be to the detriment of the weaker parties, who are in a position of non-moral inferiority, but who might have justice on their side, if it were to have any constraining effect. Thus, from a utilitarian point of view, I want to argue, the importance of the efficacy of appeals to justice, so far considered, is primarily that they sometimes benefit weaker parties.

With this conclusion in mind, we can ask, what principles of justice might, if socially efficacious, benefit weaker parties. And I think that at least a partial answer is obvious. First, those which constrain the most oppressive uses of superior power--what we would generally call respect for human rights. There may be exceptions to this as a generalization, for the use of terrorist tactics may enhance the power of a small dissident force to disrupt the normal life of a government in power, but in general the party with greater military and police power is benefited by unrestrained use of force without regard for human rights. And it seems clear to me that constraints on such use of power generally reduce suffering and would be supported by utilitarian theory. Thus, one form of justice is respect for such rights. Second, with regard to the justice of the outcome of a dispute, with regard to what is called distributive justice, the weaker party is benefited by principles which promote equality--taking away from the stronger party and promoting the weaker. Thus, the weaker would benefit from something approximating the general conception of justice which John Rawls defends: "All social primary goods--liberty and opportunity, income and wealth, and the bases of self-respect--are to be distributed equally unless unequal distribution of any or all of these goods is to the advantage of the least favored."[6]

Rawls is concerned with the justice of social institutions within a single society, but the conception can be applied to the justice of conflict resolutions and on an international scale. In a conflict, the weaker party to the conflict is normally the weaker in these kinds of primary social goods. Thus, any efficacy of moral appeal to justice which tends towards equal distribution except when unequal distribution is to the advantage of the least favored would be of benefit to the weaker party in the dispute.

Now the question to be raised is whether utilitarianism has any grounds for supporting such a theory of justice, and I think that there is a clear answer to this. It is based on the principle of diminishing marginal utility.

If it were possible to produce happiness or to eliminate unhappiness directly, then distribution might not matter to a utilitarian except as a means to the greatest long-term maximization of net happiness. But it isn't possible in most instances to produce happiness directly. What a social policy can accomplish is at best to produce the usual means to happiness: security of person and of life prospects, opportunities to fulfill one's goals, a decent standard of living, and things like that. Thus, what Rawls calls social primary goods--liberty and opportunity, wealth and income, and so on--are the means to happiness by which a social policy can seek to implement the utilitarian goal of promoting happiness. Having increments of these normally increases happiness, but it does not do so in accordance with a straight linear scale. In classical economics, the marginal utility of something is the ability of an additional unit of it to satisfy human wants--i.e., to be the means to happiness or the elimination of unhappiness. The Principle of Diminishing Marginal Utility recognizes the phenomenon that as larger quantities of something are possessed, an additional unit has less ability to satisfy wants, because there are fewer or less acute wants left to be satisfied. Thus three persons with an annual income of $30,000 each could be expected, other things equal, to have a sum total of happiness greater than two with $20,000 and one with $50,000. The last $2 in the possession of the person with $50,000 would be meeting less acute needs than if they were in the possession of the two with $20,000 each, and so on back to equality. I would claim that this is true not just of wealth and income but with all of the social primary goods which Rawls identifies: an additional increment of liberty or opportunity is more beneficial to those with limited liberty or opportunity than to those who already have extensive liberty and opportunity. This is an empirical principle which is subject to revision in the light of experiment, and there may be special circumstances in which it does not hold, but I think that it is evident from common experience that it is generally true. And, if so, the utilitarian has grounds from supporting principles which promote equality, and, in particular, principles of justice which promote the cause of the weaker party to a dispute. I conclude that there is a general coincidence between the utilitarian goal of promoting the greatest happiness and principles of justice which are egalitarian except when inegalitarian policies will result in benefits for the worst off. The egalitarian principle and its exception are both instances of seeking to make the worst-off as well off as possible, a goal which in game theory is called a "maximin" strategy--making the worst outcome as good as possible. So I shall henceforth refer to this egalitarian principle with its exception as a "maximin" principle.

This conclusion raises a question of motivation. If the principle of justice appealed to is one which benefits the weaker party, why should the stronger party ever be motivated to be constrained by it? This is a large qustion, and I can only sketch the beginning of an answer. First, the constraint may be motivated indirectly by the opinion of third parties. If the principle is accepted in society at large, or by world opinion, the unfavorable sentiment of public or world opinion may be enough to limit injustice. Second, the agent may have been socialized in an environment with this sentiment of justice held by the public at large. If so, it may be internalized in the consciousness of an agent, so that the agent accepts the principle as one of justice and is constrained by it, even when contrary to self-interest. And third, the utilitarian foundation for the principle may be recognized as reasonable: since happiness is valuable and unhappiness disvaluable wherever it occurs, and because diminishing marginal utility is an evident fact which leads to a maximin principle of justice. This is obviously not a complete account of possible motivation, but it does indicate that efficacy of a maximin principle of justice is not totally implausible. The claim is not being made that it always constrains domineering power, but that it may directly or indirectly work to provide some constraint upon brute force.

So far, our conclusion is that a maximin principle of justice would be supported by utilitarianism. But there is another role which principles of justice play in conflict resolution which complicates this conclusion. Earlier I postponed discussion of appeal to justice by a mediator or third party as a basis for negotiated settlement, but I indicated that it may function as a claim that each side is getting what it deserves. If the basis of just desert is merely the maximin principle to make the worst-off party as well off as possible, there would be nothing to be granted to the better-off party. Justice would always be one-sided, and if so it would not have some of its recognized social efficacy in conflict resolution. In arguing earlier for the maximin principle, I said that it was at least a partial answer to the question of what principles of justice follow from utilitarian arguments, and now I think that we need to recognize that it is only a partial answer. Another line of utilitarian argument leads to principles of desert based on past action, and another line of utilitarian argument leads to property rights, in the most general sense of that expression, and either or both of these may serve to support the stronger party in a dispute. Just to concentrate upon property rights, they are a source of security, which is one of the most important means to happiness and the elimination of unhappiness. As such, they may be deserving of some moral support as well as strictly juridical or armed enforcement, and to some extent, although I think it would be much the weaker, this argument may apply to corporate and national claims to property as well as personal claims. Just which property rights promote the general happiness and which interfere with it is a large question. To answer it is a huge task of utilitarian social philosophy, requiring some guiding principles which I cannot provide and requiring detailed criticism of legislative decisions, court interpretations, and executive policies as they arise, to be done in the light of the best economic and social theory available, in order that utilitarianism be applied to the real world. Thus, the application of utilitarian social philosophy is no simple task.

Macalester College

NOTES

1. Jeremy Bentham wrote, *"Natural rights* is simple nonsense: natural and imprescriptible rights, rhetorical nonsense — nonsense upon stilts." *Anarchical Fallacies, Works,* Vol. II, ed. by Bowring (1834).

2. *The Structure of Scientific Revolutions* (University of Chicago Press, 1962), Chapter II.

3. For an exploration of this, see Alasdair MacIntyre, *After Virtue* (University of Notre Dame Press, 1981).

4. See, for example, Alan Ryan, *John Stuart Mill* (Pantheon Books, 1970), Chapter XII.

5. I have conceded this point, but also defended some derivative principles of utilitarian justice in "Justice and Utility," *Moral Philosophy: Classic Texts and Contemporary Problems,* edited by Joel Feinberg and Henry West (Dickenson, 1977).

6. *A Theory of Justice* (Harvard University Press, 1971), p. 303.

SOCIAL PHILOSOPHY, NATIONAL SOCIALISM, AND THE SCARCITY SOCIETY

George J. Stein

A distinctive characteristic of National Socialism as a philosophical and ideological system was its biopolitics. National Socialist biopolitics informed all aspects of the Nazi era, from the social goals of the movement to the brutal means selected to obtain those goals. The distinctive characteristics of Nazi biopolitics were an assumption of physical or material scarcity as a constant threat to the material development and national or racial survival of the German breeding population and the assumption that competition among breeding populations was the dynamic of all processes of physical nature.

Hitler developed his ideas on the basis of German Social Darwinism as early as 1925.[1] Basing his views on those of one of Germany's leading biological scientists of the turn-of-the-century, Ernst Haeckel and Haeckel's followers in the Monist League,[2] Hitler illustrated the radical assumptions of the new biopolitics in a very instructive discussion of the interrelationship of biology and social policy. In chapter four of Volume One of Mein Kampf, Hitler analyzed the situation facing Germany from the perspective of scarcity rather than from the assumption of potential abundance common to liberal capitalist and Marxist social philosophy.[3] Hitler recognized that continued population growth within, to use the modern term, the limited carrying capacity of the German ecosystem could result only in increasing misery and ultimate starvation. Hitler considered four possible policy responses to the potential population/resource disequilibrium; three would be rejected.

The first policy option would be the obvious restriction of population growth to a size which could be sustained within the limits of the available ecosystem. This "steady state" model could be an acceptable response only if other communities could be induced to restrict their population growth. Other communities, especially Germany's neighbors, showed little likelihood of adopting a policy of population control and, consequently, reducing their eventual need to make demands on the resource base now inhabited by Germans. As the survival of a breeding population is a fundamental law of nature, it would have been "unnatural" to commit genetic suicide through population control. Or, in the words of a contemporary American biologist: "in a finite world--and no other is available to us --a breeding war works toward the competitive exclusion of the slower breeding group."[4]

The second policy option for addressing the needs of an increasing demand for resources resulting from continuous population growth would have been to increase the product or yield from available resources through modern technology. Again, Hitler saw that there are physical limits to resource extraction. Only so much fertilizer or so much technology can be applied to a fixed resource base. Only so many cattle can be run on any limited commons. Sooner or later, Hitler observed, "hunger becomes the eternal companion" of a community tied to its own resource base.

The third policy option, and that favored by modern liberal capitalist societies, would have been to recognize the interdependence of modern nations and, through technological or scientific specialization, purchase the needed food and resources through international trade. This rational or civilized response was rejected because the physical survival of a political community is too important to be placed at risk by becoming dependent on unpredictable other nations for vital resources. The devastation caused Germany by the French and Belgian occupation of the Ruhr coal region to extract "reparations" and permanently cripple German development was too fresh a memory to be ignored.

The fourth policy option was, of course, war; war justified as the natural right of any community to secure for itself the food, fuel, resources, and living space needed for survival as a national culture or breeding population. That Germany transformed itself into a collective, authoritarian, and elitist community in the name of a biopolitics of blood solidarity and national survival is evidence enough of the power of a social philosophy based on scarcity and the natural right to breed. The National Socialist social policies of racialism, militaristic/technological expansion, and corporate solidarity were a direct and logical consequence of a social philosophy of scarcity and freedom to breed.

Even the virulent anti-semitism of the Nazi era followed, not from "traditional" German anti-semitism, but as a necessary and logical conclusion of Nazi biopolitics. As the basis for the national or racial struggle for survival of a breeding population is the physical or territorial ecosystem, the Jews were seen as a special problem. Unlike, say, the Poles or Russians whose land could be contested and conquered as a necessity of territorial expansion, the Jews, lacking a land of their own, were of necessity seen as parasites whose sole means of survival was to live off the productive forces of their host countries. Thus, the Jews were seen as internationalists who sought to weaken the national consciousness of their hosts and, of course, committed to the promiscuous bastardization of race-mixing for others while keeping themselves intact as a breeding culture. Again, a social philosophy with a biopolitics of scarcity and breeding competition was seen to require, logically, a social policy of the removal of the Jewish parasite from the body of the healthy host.

In a real sense, the biopolitics of scarcity appropriated by National Socialism as both philosophic ground and pragmatic policy was totally false. It was an empirical fiction, for in no real sense could Germany or Europe be seen, in the early part of this century, to be in any serious danger from a scarcity of natural resources. Nor was Germany in any danger of exceeding the carrying capacity of its ecosystemic base. The entire social philosophy of National Socialism based on an assumption of scarcity must be seen as an act of willful self-delusion. While empirically, then, the National Socialist era must be seen to have been based on an hypothesis contrary to fact, can National Socialist social philosophy be viewed as a "thought experiment," a premature and outrageous experiment in the social policies of a true Age of Scarcity?

One of the most interesting questions of scientific or social theory is "what must the world be like for the theory describing it to be true?" That is, if we lived in a universe of spells, demons, and magic where physical reality could be transformed at whim, then "science" just could not be used. Science, despite any virtues of rationality, coherence, parsimony, etc., would just be useless. It would not be "true." If America were not a fairly stable political, social, and economic system based on a fairly widely shared consensus, social or behavioral research would be almost impossible. The experience of social scientists working in a "foreign" culture where, for example, one does not always reply forthrightly to questions from strangers, illustrates the need for a certain kind of social reality before certain kinds of scientific theory can be employed in a useful or accurate fashion. In the present case, the question becomes "what must the world be like for the social policies recommended by most modern social philosophies to be 'true'?" Or, to put it differently, "if the world is changing away from the world assumed by the majority of contemporary social philosophies, must not the assumptions and the putative social policies of those philosophical systems be called into question?"

Whatever else human politics may be, it is at least the means by which human communities attempt to address the basic problem of the survival of the community. Every human society must attempt to provide food, fuel, and establish conditions favorable for successful biological reproduction of its members. Failure results in the decline or extinction of the community as a society, albeit not necessarily the extinction of each individual member of that society.

Whatever assumptions about the nature of reality or whatever values a society holds as it orders itself for action in history, all human societies must make some judgment, either explicit or tacit, about the scarcity or abundance of those factors which affect the quest for food, fuel, and conditions favorable for successful biological reproduction. All human societies, then, have a biopolitics. Most human societies, historically, have had a biopolitics which assumed, correctly in most cases, that a scarcity of resources was the reality.[5] Equality of access to scarce resources was very rarely adopted by human groups and the "primitive communism" beloved of Marxist social philosophy must be seen to have the same ontological status as the "Garden of Eden." Hierarchy, oppression of the many by the few, and, in essence, differential access to the resources needed for successful reproduction have been the qualities which distinguished most human communities. The general function of politics has been to distribute scarcity in a way which assures, minimally, the continued existence of the community as community (q. v. Aristotle, Politics).

The values held by most post-Renaissance social philosophies, such as a belief in reason as the key to social and scientific progress, political liberalism manifested as liberty, equality and human solidarity, private capitalist growth in material well-being, and the inviolable dignity of the individual human person, all rest ultimately on a biopolitics which assumes the potential, if not the actuality, of cornucopian abundance. The existence of an abundance of resources is absolutely central to the liberal doctrines of John Locke and Adam Smith.[6] Any justification for the right of individual persons to appropriate to themselves resources from the commons of the physical planet can only be made by assuming that such appropriation threatens neither any other individual with diminished resources needed for successful reproduction nor the existence of the community as community. Any labor theory of value, common to capitalist or socialist alike, rests on a similar assumption of infinite raw resources to be subjected to human transformation. The pursuit of life, liberty, and happiness-as-property by free, equal, self-regarding individuals must assume that such individualistic pursuing does not deny the potential for successful pursuing by the next person. Very few social philosophers committed to the free life style of mixing one's labor with raw material nature seem to have noticed that Locke himself recognized the tentative nature of the assumption of abundance. Locke knew that such appropriation from the planetary commons by free individuals could be justified as a value only so long as "there was still enough, and as good left" for the next man.[7] Locke feared what most modern social philosophy has forgotten; that Hobbes was right. Every person has a fundamental natural right to attempt to gain access to those resources needed to preserve his own life and, in a condition of scarcity where one man's gain could imply another man's peril, every man is potentially the enemy of every other man. Only the mighty Leviathan could allocate scarcity in an authoritative fashion within a community. Between communities, the likelihood was war.

Modern Western society and modern social philosophers have been lucky. The world was like the theory said it was. Vast amounts of "free" fuel lay in the ground permitting the transformation of other physical reality into usable energy and food. Vast amounts of "empty" land lay open to receive the exploding populations of free, self-regarding individuals. Whole national communities could be organized and come to understand themselves as actors in history as having the natural rights to life, liberty, and the pursuit of happiness-as-property-in-things. Social policies based on abundance became mere domestic squabbles over the happy division of an ever increasing fund of food, fuel, and conditions for successful biological reproduction. Most civilized nations could even afford to encourage continual population growth through public health and positive social welfare. If anything, the Marxists represent the very essence of modern social philosophy in their commitment to the abolition of scarcity and the conquest of the kingdom of necessity through human labor. They differ from liberal capitalist social philosophers only in their view that this upward march of humanity should be directed by the community in the interests of the whole community and, that the benefits, food, fuel, and conditions appropriate for successful reproduction, be actually distributed among those whose material labor makes the great transformation possible.

The game, however, may be over. And, to tell the truth, for millions of our fellow human beings who did not have the good fortune to be born into our modern Western society, there was never any game at all. For most people on the planet, scarcity is not an assumption in a social philosophy, it is a daily fact. And, for them, social policies which attempt to contribute to the peaceful resolution of social conflicts but which continue to hold the assumption of potential cornucopian abundance as the end of policy are a cruel hoax. The very question "how should we decide what percentage of our resources to devote to defense versus aid to the poor?" illustrates too well the dilemma of modern social philosophy.

The general lack of serious and sustained attention by social philosophers to appropriate social policies for an Age of Scarcity, either the one that now exists for many of the people of the planet or the one that may need to be faced by the Euro-American societies, is easy to understand. The problem is both philosophical and political or structural. The philosophical problem has already been implied; that is, the basic assumption of most contemporary social philosophy can recognize only relative scarcity. Relative scarcity is either merely a matter of ordinary politics to be addressed by a redivision of a growing pie, as when labor unions want more for their members, or as a temporary disequilibrium of supply and demand. If the price is right, the scarce "good" will somehow appear out of the great transformation possible of the infinite resources of the planet and "scarcity" will vanish. To use an idea favored by historians of science, modern social theory is equipped to recognize relative scarcity as a "puzzle" and "solve" it. <u>Absolute</u> scarcity is an "anomaly" which can be neither admitted nor addressed without a fundamental change in the "theory."

The political and structural obstacles to a serious rethinking of the options for social policy in an Age of Scarcity derive generally from the role that continued growth of both population and standard of living or demands for additional resource consumption per capita have played in modern society. The belief in growth and the actual delivering on that promise have provided an important goal for individual effort, have provided a general policy goal on which to build a social consensus, have contributed to political and social stability and, perhaps less well appreciated, have provided continuing legitimacy for the existence of an elite, the relative unequal distribution of wealth, and the philosophical or ideological justifications for both. After all, as long as I am getting "more" it matters little if my boss is getting "a lot more." As long as social policy is defined as fair access or equal opportunity to an increased share of the spoils, social solidarity can be maintained. For a social policy defined as "due process" which equates the will of a plurality of partial interests with the general will or the common good, an ever increasing "output" is required to maintain peaceful resolution of conflicts. For an elite leadership in a democratic and representative polity which can only attain or maintain its position of leadership by promising and delivering an ever increasing range of goods and services to an ever growing diversity of demands, an ever increasing "output" is required to maintain legitimacy. In essence, modern social philosophy and its social policies can be maintained only by continuing to assert a philosophical outlook and social practice currently at odds with most of the people of the planet and increasingly at odds with the physical and social realities of its own ecumene.

Many discussions of a philosophic or social response to the

issues raised by the possibility of a scarcity society often resolve themselves into a call for a "religious" change of heart or some form of utopian fantasy. Leaving aside the advocates of "no growth" whose social policies would freeze the status quo and relegate much of the planet to the status of living folk museums, and the advocates of space colonialization, fusion power, or other magic bullet technological saviors, most social philosophers call for something like a Zen Buddhist ethic of renunciation where we are to "walk softly on the Earth" or a grand system of redistribution whereby we would all eat granola and give our cattle feed to the Africans rather than selling it to the Russians. Now it must be admitted that the soft walkers and the redistributionists might be right; perhaps we "ought" to adopt pre-modern values like love of neighbor or the curiously medieval notion that it is better to suffer evil than do it. It may be a bad bargain to gain the world and lose one's soul. On the other hand, one of the great Renaissance founders of modern social philosophy reminds us that "how we live is so far removed from how we ought to live, that he who abandons what is done for what ought to be done, will rather learn to bring out his own ruin than his preservation."[8]

The starting point, then, of any philosophical discussion of social policies appropriate to an Age of Scarcity is the recognition that the citizens of the United States, Europe and Japan, the rulers of Russia and China, and the Westernized elites in the Third World are not going to begin to walk softly on the Earth or come to any consensus on the "ought" of redistributing either access to resources or outputs of resource transformations. Social and political "facts" can be intractable. Thus, any social philosophy appropriate to an Age of Scarcity must recognize the likelihood that conflict over real or perceived scarce resources will be the central issue of social policy in the future. Politics may need to be re-recognized as the means human groups use to "adjust" the man/resource balance within the context of neo-Darwinian evolution. What would such a social philosophy look like?

The core question of ethics is how the individual chooses or ought to choose to live as an individual. Social ethics focuses on how the individual and the society in which the individual lives do or ought to relate. Social philosophy, then, assumes the existence of society or a community. If, following Aristotle, to live well one must first have life, then social philosophy must be concerned with the life of the community. Living, that is, the provision of adequate food, fuel, and conditions appropriate for successful biological reproduction so that the community as community continues to exist, is the first order of business, the "end" or "function" of social policy. Ethics has discovered that individual persons may choose, for perfectly rational reasons such as individual reproductive success or simple willfulness, to behave in a manner which, from the perspective of the community, is seen, often correctly, as greedy and selfish. Ethics, to be sure, has also discovered altruistic behavior. Social policy, however, must discover a way to protect and advance the interests of the community when the individual members of the community are as likely to be as selfish as they are altruistic.

Among the various things humans do is to breed increased numbers of human beings. For whatever reason, human populations seem to grow. In fact, human populations grow to "fit" the resources available in the form of food, fuel, etc. Humans have evolved the ability to alter, change, and transform their environments, from settled agriculture to the very latest technology, to provide more resources. The great population explosions followed each new technology and human numbers were "bred up" to the limits of available resources. As the limits of resources began to be approached, "poverty" and all that entails began to affect first some, then more, members of the breeding community. Poverty, it seems, may be a consequence not only of oppression, but of population growth as well.

Within a social community on an isolated island, the response to the advent of poverty consequent upon numbers or demand could be to limit the numbers and redistribute resources to those willing to limit their number of children or to restrain their demands. The community could continue to exist so long as total numbers and total demand did not exceed the carrying capacity of the island ecosystem. An increase in numbers or an increase in demand would split the community, first into factions, ultimately into the war of all against all.

While this island Earth is one interdependent ecosystem, it is not a community. We are divided into countless competing tribes, races, and national cultures. The social and political reality is that there is no world government, no mighty Leviathan, no world consensus on the need to limit either numbers or demand. While humankind is potentially a biological unity, the reality is a great diversity of more or less discrete breeding populations. Numbers and demand increase to consume available resources and, in a world divided into discrete populations, the slower breeding group or the less demanding group relinquishes its "share" of resources to the faster breeding or more greedy groups. Whatever one might wish to argue "ought" to be responsible behavior and social policy, it would appear that it "is" the case that humans have evolved in a way which results in numbers and demands increasing to consume available resources.

A social philosophy appropriate to an Age of Scarcity which lacks a world consensus or government with sufficient authority and power to both regulate numbers and redistribute resources must consider the possibility that an individual nation or breeding community has the duty to follow whatever social policies it needs, both domestically and in its "foreign" relations, to assure access to sufficient food, fuel, and conditions for successful reproduction so that its members can continue to live as a community. Lacking a world government, no nation can be said to have any moral or legal responsibility for the well-being of any other discrete breeding community unless it perceives it in its own interest to take such an interest. To illustrate with a current issue. As the United States does not have the moral authority or legal responsibility to take those measures needed to bring Mexican numbers and demand into conformity with Mexican resources or carrying capacity, the United States cannot be said to have any social or ethical responsibility to absorb those Mexicans who cannot be sustained at the level of consumption they might wish for themselves within the limits of the Mexican ecosystem. If the United States chooses to act as a "safety valve" while Mexico, as a sovereign breeding community, takes steps to control numbers and demand or increase "output," it might be a prudent policy. If Mexico fails to take these measures, it is quite simply accurate to say that the Mexican breeding population is "at war" with the American breeding population over access to scarce resources. Lacking a world government, the United

States as a social community whose function or purpose is to assure access to resources for its population is free to take whatever steps a community under attack might take.

Is this National Socialist thinking? Of course it is. The point is that Mexican immigration, American support for South Africa to maintain access to strategic metals, or the development of a "rapid deployment force" to maintain access to Middle Eastern oil fields, all illustrate the politics of scarcity. The failure of social philosophy to develop rational and humane approaches to conflict resolution which recognize the reality of real or perceived scarcity on a global basis where "as much and as good" is no longer available for the next man threatens to leave the National Socialist response to scarcity as the chief philosophical option to inform social policy. Surely we can do better than that.

Miami University, Ohio

NOTES

1. Daniel Gasman, *The Scientific Origins of National Socialism*. New York: American Elsevier, 1971.

2. David H. DeGrood, *Haeckel's Theory of the Unity of Nature*. New Jersey: Humanities Press, 1982.

3. Adolf Hitler, *Mein Kampf*. Boston: Houghton Mifflin, 1943.

4. Garrett Hardin, *Promethean Ethics*. Seattle: University of Washington Press, 1980.

5. William Ophuls, *Ecology and the Politics of Scarcity*. San Francisco: W.H. Freeman, 1977.

6. C.B. Macpherson, *The Political Theory of Possessive Individualism*. Oxford: Clarendon Press, 1962.

7. John Locke, *Two Treatises of Government*. Cambridge, England: The University Press, 1960.

8. Paul Colinvaux, *The Facts of Nations: A biological theory of history*. New York: Simon and Schuster, 1980.

USING FOOD AS A WEAPON

William Aiken

American agriculture is drastically overproductive and it has been for several decades. Since the 1930s diverse policies have evolved to alleviate the adverse economic effects of this overproduction: from price subsidies and governmental purchase, to land banking and, most recently, the Payment in Kind (PIK) program. The most effective way to deal with surplus, however, has been to expand into foreign markets either through "trade" or, when necessary, through concessionary "aid." The expansion into foreign markets has not only helped to eliminate surplusses, contain subsidy and storage costs, and stabilize domestic prices, it has also proven to be quite profitable for agribusiness. In the last decade there has been an additional impetus helping to promote this strategy-- the need to substantially increase our exports in order to offset the unhealthy trade deficit that higher oil prices and Americans' preference for foreign consumer items has created. Hence the government has endorsed and complied with the expansion of food trade.

The Russian grain embargo dramatically called attention to the political aspects of food trade. By explicitly subordinating economic advantage to political objectives, President Carter inadvertently opened the public's eyes to the complexity of the food trade and the extent to which American agribusiness had become dependent on foreign markets. Throughout the 1960s the public had viewed United States' involvement in international food trade, especially the "aid" programs (called by fancy names like Food Aid, and, later, Food for Peace), almost entirely as "humanitarian" projects in which America, the "Breadbasket of the World," was benevolently "feeding the world's hungry." This image was promoted by agribusiness and even the U.S.D.A. even though the economic and political advantages were the prime factors in developing these programs. Food trade was being used as a political and economic tool of diplomacy even though the public was largely unaware of this. It wasn't until the Russian grain embargo that the public began to see and to ask questions about the propriety of using food as a weapon. The overt clash between the economic policy of expanding trade and the political objective of regulating trade to punish the Soviets began to awaken the public to an issue that had been seething for years--to what extent and for what purposes should food trade and aid be used to promote political objectives. The food weapon had been an issue for some time among environmentalists, Neo-malthusians, zero-population growth advocates, agribusiness interests, those critical of and those supportive of American involvement in LDC development, various factions in the U.S.D.A. and the Pentagon and C.I.A., the farm lobby, the relief organizations, and just about everyone else knowledgeable of the international food situation. But when it "hit" the public it caused confusion and fervor.

This issue is precisely the kind of social policy issue that exhibits deep and perhaps irreconcilable value conflicts. It is one that cannot be solved by seeking the popular consensus since there is none. It is not one for which a public opinion poll will be of much use since the public is often sorely uninformed on the issues involved. (I am reminded of a country and western song which came out not long after one of OPEC's embargoes that suggested "Food for Crude" as if Saudi Arabia could not buy grain elsewhere.) It is not very likely to be solved by the Washington experts since, depending on the department to which they are attached, they will differ on the varying importance which should be attached to the possible economic, strategic, and symbolic gains resulting from a specific wielding of the food weapon. Nor is it likely to be solved by a satisfactory compromise between varying interests since the divergence of objectives is too great (for example between the grain exporters and the Neo-malthusians). Thus, it is the kind of issue on which some philosophical analysis, reflection and guidance may prove to be instructive.

Furthermore, this is the time to do this reflection because even though the food weapon issue is on the back burner in Washington right now, due to President Regan's preference for more "direct" weapons (such as the installation of missiles, the deployment of military advisors, and the giving of military aid) to achieve his objectives, it is likely to arise again, especially in our dealings in Central America since the Congress is increasingly blocking President Regan's preferred methods. Even though the President is a general advocate of free trade, his attempt to block the Soviet gas pipeline by embargo demonstrates his willingness to use commodity weapons to achieve what he considers go be an advantage. So an effort to get a clear understanding of the "food weapon" now may at least help us to see what is involved in adopting such a policy and it may help to prevent the careless implementation of a misguided policy in the future.

How can food be used as a weapon? Of course food is not a weapon in the sense of being an implement of destruction. The expression "food weapon" is a metaphor for the intentional use of trade in food substances as a means of gaining political influence. It is a weapon only in the sense of being a tool for punishing, manipulating, exploiting, or influencing others for some political objective. Unlike "real" weapons which work by directly threatening or causing harm to persons or property, the food weapon works indirectly by frustrating the expectations, wants or needs of the victims. It is designed to cause, exacerbate, discontinue or fail to alleviate a shortage (real or felt) of food. In wielding this weapon one foresees and intends a hardship to result from the scarcity and this hardship is the "harm" that will either serve to punish the victim or render the victim vulnerable to the manipulation of his or her decisions and actions. But for this weapon to work, the hardship must be substantial. A commodity weapon can only work in conditions of scarcity since without scarcity there can be no leverage. The scarcity may be created (for example, by blockade), exacerbated (for example, by creating a trade dependency through "dumping" subsidized grain in order to undercut local production and then curtailing or withholding further shipments), or it may be found (as when a drought or a civil war or crop failure drastically reduces the available supply). In order for the scarcity to be substantial enough to make the weapon effective, there must be no other (easily available) source of the commodity. Thus for the food weapon to be a weapon, other dealers in foodstuffs must either cooperate with the wielder, or be charging prices that exceed the capability of the country suffering the shortage. It would be useless to try to manipulate a country by refusing to trade if others are willing to trade without similar conditions.

All of these features are common to commodity weapons in general, from the sale of oil, to arms, to pipeline equipment, to Coca-Cola and blue jeans. Unless there is a politically motivated, intentional attempt to frustrate expectations of attaining a scarce good, there can be no "weapon." But the food weapon differs from other commodity weapons in one essential aspect; the scarcity level has very narrow limits of tolerability. Since food is necessary for life itself, a scarcity can cause severe hardship rather quickly. The standard ways of coping with a scarcity are substitution, abstinence, and conservation. But these don't work very well for food shortages. Unlike blue jeans, basic food stuffs are not substitutable and unlike Coca-Cola, they cannot be done without. Attempts at conservation are effective only if the general level of nutrition exceeds the basic minimum. Yet in virtually all countries vulnerable to the food weapon (those suffering substantial shortages) there is both a maldistribution of wealth and purchasing power and a significant portion of the population already surviving at or below the subsistence level. Even though the rich and well to do in any country will not go hungry no matter how hard times are, the most vulnerable (the poor, young and powerless) will feel the adverse effects of conservation efforts soonest and most severely. Even minor attempts at conservation (without redistribution) will drastically affect their well being. This special link between food and essential needs and the fact of the narrowness of the range of toleration of scarcity are what make the food weapon potentially a powerful tool for coercion and manipulation. However, it should be stressed that the "food weapon" used against impoverished nations does not have the same potential effect that the "oil weapon" has against oil-importing, industrialized nations since the hardship imposed is disproportionately borne by the poor and since this hardship is less likely to disrupt the entire economy (even though it may exact more lives).

In using the food weapon you are attempting to coerce or manipulate political leaders to abide your will by knowingly acting so as to indirectly cause (or at least permit) a scarcity level of food severe enough to threaten those who are most vulnerable to suffer from want of food. What this boils down to is: using the suffering of the innocent to manipulate the powerful. This point is important because much of the debate over the food weapon seems to confuse the victims with the ones you are trying to manipulate. The targets of the weapon (those who suffer the hardship) are not the same as those toward whom you are hostile (the political leaders). It is only by evoking a spurious notion of collective liability that these two can be equated. Knowing who the food weapon "hurts" is important if one is to properly evaluate the acceptability of this policy.

Is there anything wrong with this use of food trade as a weapon? There are two ways to assess the food weapon. First, one can treat it as a morally neutral means and judge the propriety of a particular use by assessing the merit of the end or objective being sought by its use. In addition to national interest objectives, there are broader international goals for which it could be used; for instance to enhance international economic stability or cooperation in solving global problems such as overpopulation, natural resource depletion, and environmental damage. Or it may be wielded for humanitarian goals such as to enhance quality of life, protect human rights, or spur reforms for more equitable distribution of wealth within the country against which it is wielded. Many of the conflicts in values that have arisen over the use of the food weapon stem from disagreement over the legitimacy of the goals pursued. Support for population control (no more food without birth control) ran high in the 1970s. Support for environmental protection runs high in the 1980s. And of course, winning friends and punishing enemies in the third world goes hand in hand with our military interests. Debate over the worthiness and advisability of these goals, though ultimately related to using the food weapon as a means to attain them, is a separate topic. But even granting that some of these goals are worthwhile does not settle the question as to whether the food weapon is an effective means for attaining them.

The second way to assess the use of food as a weapon is to address the propriety of the means itself. Is there anything wrong with using A's hardship to manipulate B to abide your will? The answer to this question depends very much upon the extent to which you caused the scarcity. Indirectly causing harm to innocent persons by intentionally causing a scarcity is wrong for the same reason that directly causing harm to innocent persons (for example, bombing a school) is wrong. If there are moral duties at all, the duty of non-malficence (which prohibits the intentional harming of innocent persons) is one, and it is considered the most stringent duty by virtually all moral theories. The purported justification for causing this harm in both the case of terrorism and intentionally causing life-threatening scarcity is that this harm is justified to the extent that it successfully coerces or manipulates others so as to attain some good goal. But this justification for overriding the *prima facie* duty of non-malficence falls prey to another moral criticism. Such action violates another moral duty which is staunchly upheld by both deontologists and rule-utilitarians, the duty to treat persons as ends in themselves. So both the aspects of "harming" and "using" cause moral problems, and when combined they make it difficult to justify using the food weapon in a way that causes the scarcity.

But typically, the scarcity which makes the food weapon possible is found, not created. Though one's actions may exacerbate it, one has not caused it. What is wrong with fanning the flames a little and then exploiting the situation for your advantage? Even though you know that your actions will result in increased suffering of innocents, still technically you are not causing harm by failing to alleviate hardship unless your terms are met. Is it permissible to use innocent persons' needs due to scarcity to manipulate others to abide your will? Kantian purists may still object that this is to use persons merely as means and thus is an unacceptable disregard for their autonomy. And many who oppose the food weapon in principle object to this playing of politics with persons' lives on grounds that such bargaining becomes shameful when the stakes for some are life or death. However, since the practice is so common it would be desirable to find a stronger argument than the ones that appeal to the vague notion of treating of persons as ends in themselves or merely point out the extremity of the costs to some.

The standard move here is to challenge the moral relevance of the omission-commission distinction and suggest that intentionally refusing to alleviate suffering is as morally wrong as intentionally causing suffering. Thus it is not merely the "use" aspect that makes it wrong, it is also the "cause" aspect reinterpreted to include "inaction" as a causal factor (which reintroduces the duty of non-malificence). Causing harm to manipulate, e.g., terrorism, would be on a par with failing to alleviate so as to manipulate, the food weapon. I happen to be one of those who find the omission-commission distinction to be of questionable moral relevance (or more accurately, I do not find that omissions are entirely permissible though perhaps not as wrongful as commissions). But for the sake of argument, I will grant that the exploiting of scarcity and the use of innocents' suffering to manipulate others is, in principle, permissible. This allows the food weapon when used as a means for exploiting scarcity to be considered morally permissible.

But the story is not over yet. We must link the means (permissible by hypothesis) to the end (worthy by hypothesis). We must demonstrate that the food weapon as a tool of diplomacy can deliver, can be an effective means for attaining a political objective. If the case can be made that this tool is not very likely to be an effective means of attaining one's objective (no matter how worthy) then the conflict over the various goals for which it is being used, and the conflict over the general permissibility of the means itself will become secondary, if not moot. The most severe conflicts surrounding the food weapon can be largely resolved by being rendered irrelevant if the food weapon can be shown to be (usually) an ineffective means to attain the goal.

First, some refinements on the various uses of the food weapon must be made. A symbolic use is one designed to make a political statement to other nations. It is a public relations action designed to stress a difference in ideology or to push a point of principle. (For example, refusing to sell grain to a country whose leader we refuse to acknowledge.) A retaliatory use is backward looking; it is designed to punish a nation for past action. (An example might be Stalin's starving of the Ukraine.) A manipulatory use is forward looking; it is designed to pressure an adversary into abiding your will. The manipulative use is by far the most common. Pure cases of the retaliatory use are rare. Even though the Russian grain embargo was officially retaliatory, its real function was symbolic (to make a statement to other nations) and manipulative (to influence future Soviet action). I will grant that the food weapon can be an effective means for attaining the political objectives of making an international symbolic statement, and that it may be an effective means of retaliation (if in fact a substantial hardship results--which was not the case with the Russian grain embargo). But since these uses are peripheral to the dominant manipulative use I do not think that this concession will weaken my case that the food weapon is generally an ineffective means of attaining your objective.

To see why the food weapon is not likely to be an effective means of manipulating political leaders to abide your will, consider the following two cases.

Case 1:
I offer to save a woman's child from a burning house only if she promises to have sexual intercourse with me.

Case 2:
The United States' government refuses to continue to sponsor the selling of grain at concessionary prices to an impoverished and import-dependent nation unless it permits the installation of United States' nuclear missiles on its soil.

In both cases the distress of the sufferers (child, citizens) is being used to manipulate another (mother, political leaders). In both cases the conditions demanded are not, we shall assume, judged to be in the best interests of the one being manipulated. What is the likelihood in each case of attaining the objective by manipulation?

The attempt to exploit the mother is likely to be successful because the special relationship to the child is usually strong enough to predict a sacrifice of self-interest. But what about the second case? Organic theories of state aside, few political leaders feel such a strong bond to their citizens. Governmental leaders even of highly affluent nations can and do tolerate the suffering of their poor (and powerless) people. There is no special familial bond, and the motives of genuine benevolence or empathetic concern cannot be counted on to motivate political leaders to sacrifice what they perceive to be in their national interest. The mere fact that the poor are suffering (and stand to suffer even greater hardship) by itself is no reason for compliance.

What would motivate political leaders to "buckle under" to the manipulation? Perhaps if the scarcity threatened to provoke sufficient dissent and unrest so as to challenge the leaders' authority, power, or government itself, then they may be motivated to comply. Fear of food riots, a coup, or a revolution stemming from the scarcity might compel them to concede for the sake of retaining their power. Or they may (and this seems far more common) strengthen their security forces to suppress the dissent by force. Or, if they are clever, they can deflect the criticism onto the manipulating nation and call their people to a patriotic sacrifice to avoid being a puppet of "foreign imperialists." Political turmoil generated by food scarcity need not be (and historically has not often been) quieted by concessionary bargains with food supplying nations. Accurately predicting this response before wielding the food weapon (a requirement if the weapon is to be part of a rational policy) is dubious.

Alternatively, the leaders may "buckle under" because they (belatedly) acknowledge that the objective being foisted upon them is actually in the long term interest of their nation. Population control, military alliance, stronger economic ties, and even United States' missiles may serve the manipulated nation's interest. So the weapon in this case would be used in a somewhat paternalistic manner, to persuade the victim to realize that the conditions being demanded are actually beneficial to the manipulated as well as to the manipulator. Under these conditions political leaders would be foolish not to "buckle under" for by so doing they win doubly--their food scarcity problem is not exacerbated and additional long term advantages are obtained. Of course, if they are skilled, they will hold out for the maximum derivable advantage even at the cost of tolerating some adverse effects from the prolonged scarcity. It is not the fact of scarcity that motivates them, it is the potential advantage of the objective. So they are not "sacrificing" anything for those who suffer from the scarcity.

Or they may simply see the manipulation threat as a game of horse trading, of playing tit for tat: you obviously want something, we want the food, so let's make a deal--what do you have in mind? The conditions of the trade need not promote their nation's long term interests. Provided that the conditions do not substantially interfere with that interest and provided that they do prevent an increase of the scarcity problem, the leaders may choose to cooperate. But they can always choose not to, if the price seems too high or if the conditions begin to infringe on what they perceive to be in the interest of their nation. It is meaningful to talk about using the food weapon in this context only if we understand it as a somewhat hyperbolic expression for the advantage enjoyed by the supplier of a scarce commodity in a seller's market. But it should be noticed that there are limits to the price, beyond which the consumer won't go. The leverage is not what we would normally call coercive.

In all of these cases, the "effectiveness" of the food weapon is questionable. In the first case the outcome is highly unpredictable. In the second and third cases the coercive element has dropped out and we have a bargaining for mutual advantage. What compels the leaders in all of these cases to comply is not merely the suffering of their people due to scarcity. This they can tolerate. It is rather the possibility of a personal power loss or the prospect of benefit that motivates them to "buckle under." If this is (generally) the case then the food weapon is, at best, an unpredictable and not overly effective tool of coercion. As a bargaining chip it might be used with influential effect if used well (so as to avoid evoking a reactionary refusal) and if the terms demanded are reasonable for the one being manipulated. But this certainly takes the cutting edge off of the food "weapon."

If these reflections are accurate, then the policy implications for any contemplated future use of the food weapon are two. First, it is unwise (because unpredictable) to attempt to use the food weapon to destabilize a leader or his or her government. Second, if it is to be used effectively, the objectives sought must be ones that the manipulated nation can find to be in its national interest. But since such cases will not (I would suggest) be frequent, then food trade will not be a very useful "weapon." Since it is not likely to be a very useful weapon, and since there may well be other moral reasons which seem to make it undesirable, and since there is a sharp conflict of values over the acceptability of this weapon and thus no popular consensus supporting its use, then this weapon should (except perhaps in rare cases) be removed from our arsenal.

Chatham College

NATIONAL DEFENSE VS. SOCIAL WELFARE

James P. Sterba

Since 1980 the U.S. defense budget has increased by $116 billion or 87%. During the same time period the non-entitlement social welfare component of the budget increased by $6 billion or 11%, and the federal deficit increased by $678 billion or 74%. Are these changes morally justified?[1] In an effort to determine whether they are, I propose first to get clear about what should be the goals of both national defense and social welfare and second to compare these goals to determine whether either goal has priority over the other.

The Goal of National Defense

In the introduction to his Annual Report to the Congress for fiscal year 1984 Caspar Weinberger cited the goal of "rebuilding America's defenses" as the justification for the recent increases in the defense budget.[2] Presumably, Weinberger viewed such increases as necessary for the U.S. to achieve optimal military security. But when does a nation achieve optimal military security? Is it when it possesses
1) the most destructive and reliable weapons systems current technology can provide or
2) weapon systems that are superior in destructive capability to those of one's adversary or
3) weapon systems that are equal in destructive capability to those of one's adversary or
4) weapon systems that are capable of destroying one half of an adversary's industrial capacity and one quarter of its population or
5) weapon systems that are simply capable of delivering an extremely costly blow to one's adversary?

Now while many people today still interpret optimal military security as requiring either alternative (4) or (5) many more seem to favor alternatives (1), (2) or (3). For example, the Republican National Party Platform in 1980 endorsed alternative

(2), and at least during the first half of his term in office President Reagan seemed to favor either alternatives (1) or (2). More recently, however, Reagan seems to prefer to describe the weapon systems he favors in terms of alternative (3), although this may be more a change of rhetoric than substance.

In deciding which of these alternatives is the most morally defensible, it is important to recognize that they all purport to provide optimal military security at least in part through a policy of deterrence. The idea underlying this policy is that the weapon systems a nation possesses provides the basis for a threat to retaliate against its adversaries, and when a nation achieves optimal military security, it does so at least in part because such threats suffice to deter its adversaries from acts of aggression.

But can a nation always threaten to use the weapon systems it possesses for the purpose of deterring its adversaries? In this context, the principle that is often discussed by philosophers is the following:

> The Wrongful Threatening Principle: If an act is wrong then threatening to perform that act is also wrong.

This principle is usually interpreted to be a moral principle which rules out threatening under certain conditions. Interpreting the principle in this fashion, Gregory Kavka has argued that the principle fails to apply when threats are adopted solely to prevent the occurrence of the circumstances in which the threats would have to be carried out.[3] For Kavka the U.S. policy of threatening massive nuclear retaliation is justified provided that the U.S. threatens to retaliate with a massive use of nuclear weapons only to prevent the occurrence of those circumstances in which it would so retaliate. Unfortunately, this line of argument would also serve to justify the threats standardly employed by armed robbers! For robbers in threatening "Hand over your money or I'll shoot" usually hope to avoid just those circumstances where you don't hand over your money and they do shoot.

Now it is clear from his earlier work[4] that Kavka is primarily concerned with situations where people threaten in order to prevent an unjust offense, and certainly such motivation would typically be lacking in cases of armed robbery. However, when Kavka comments upon what is distinctive about those situations where he thinks such threatening is justified, he only refers to the effects the threats have that are independent of their actually being carried out, that is, to their "autonomous effects." But threats by armed robbers have just the same autonomous effects. Consequently, if a national policy of deterrence is not to be condemned on the basis of the Wrongful Threatening Principle, it must be for reasons other than those Kavka provides.

Now others, like Michael Walzer, have recognized the Wrongful Threatening Principle as a moral constraint on legitimate threats, but have then argued that in cases of national defense the principle can be overridden to achieve deterrence.[5] According to Walzer,

> We threaten in order not to do it, and the doing of it would be so terrible that the threat seems in comparison to be morally defensible.[6]

So presumably what Walzer would say about what distinguishes a nation's legitimate threatening from a robber's illegitimate threatening is not the presence of autonomous effects since such effects are found in both cases. Rather the cases are to be distinguished on the grounds that the beneficial autonomous effects that flow from legitimate threatening by a nation are not matched, even proportionately, by the beneficial autonomous effects that flow from the threats standardly employed by armed robbers.

Yet what Walzer and others fail to see is that there is an even stronger principle regarding threatening applicable here that renders certain threats impossible rather than immoral. That principle, which turns on the fact that threatening involves an intention to carry out the threat if the desired response is not forthcoming, is the following:

> The Impossible Threat Principle: X cannot threaten to do W if Y does Z if X expects that if Y does Z, X still will not do W.

Now it is important to recognize that many of the purported threats employed by nations to deter their adversaries fail to satisfy this principle. For example, in the case of the superpowers, it is frequently said that at least a massive counter-city nuclear strike would be so grossly immoral that probably neither the leaders of the United States nor those of the Soviet Union could conceive of themselves as carrying out such a strike even in retaliation. Yet many of those who think that this is the case, still believe that it is possible for the leaders of the superpowers to threaten each other with such a massive counter-city strike. But according to the Impossible Threat Principle this cannot occur. A nation's leaders simply cannot threaten nuclear retaliation if an adversary strikes first and yet expect that even if its adversary were to strike first, they would still not retaliate.

Needless to say, others have also thought that there was a logical flaw involved in our talk about threats, but they have failed to correctly state what the flaw is. Jonathan Schell, for example, claims that there is a contradiction at the heart of the doctrine of deterrence employed by the superpowers.[7] According to Schell, that contradiction is:

> We cannot both threaten ourselves with something and hope to avoid that same thing by making the threat.[8]

But the contradiction Schell claims to have discovered is not a contradiction at all but rather a commonplace. As we noted before, even robbers threaten harmful consequences while hoping never to have to carry out those threats. Rather what would be contradictory is not a threat coupled with a hope never to have to carry out the threat but rather a threat coupled with the expectation that one would never carry out the threat no matter what others did.

It follows that if the leaders of a nation could be brought to see that many of the weapon systems that are required under alternatives (1), (2) and (3) are unusable because of their morally unacceptable effects on innocent lives, they would not be able to threaten to use such weapons even in retaliation for a nuclear attack and, hence, they would not be able to achieve deterrence by such means.

Certainly this result should be surprising to many strategists in the field. For the logical connection between threatening and the expectation of possible use has not been generally appreciated. For strategists in this area have thought that nations could pile up weapon systems for the purpose of deterrence by threatening, at the same time that their leaders had no expectation of using those weapons in an all-out attack.

Yet once it is recognized that deterrence by threatening would have to be achieved with respect to weapon systems that the leaders of nations could conceive of themselves as using, the grounds for interpreting optimal military security as requiring a version of (4) or (5) becomes evident. For only if weapons procurement is limited to one or the other of these objectives would it appear to be possible for leaders of nations to actually threaten to use the weapons they have procured.

Now it might be objected that although leaders of nations could not actually threaten to use all the weapon systems they would have procured under alternatives (1), (2) and (3), they could still use such procurement to secure nuclear deterrence by means of a bluff.[9] However, there is no need to resort to bluffing to secure the desired degree of deterrence since the weapon systems required by versions (4) or (5) would suffice to provide the deterrence that is required. In fact, as I have argued at length elsewhere, there is no need, under present conditions, even to threaten to use such weapon systems to achieve the required deterrence.[10] Consequently, it would be a mistake to add a totally unnecessary bluff to a presently unnecessary threat to achieve the deterrence we require. Accordingly, the legitimate goal of national defense should interpret optimal military security so as to require the less costly alternatives (4) or (5) rather than the more costly alternatives (1), (2) or (3).

The Goal of Social Welfare

Turning to the goal of social welfare, there are at least two seemingly competing moral perspectives that purport to specify the nature and moral force of the goal of social welfare. One perspective, which we can call the libertarian perspective, holds that the only basic rights that people have are negative rights and, hence, no one has an underived positive right to social welfare but only negative rights to noninterference with one's person and one's resources, surplus or otherwise. Thus, according to this perspective, the goal of social welfare is basically a supererogatory goal and, hence, it cannot take precedence over other social goals founded on people's rights. The other perspective holds that everyone has an underived positive right to basic welfare which overrides or puts limits upon the negative ownership rights of persons with surplus resources. According to this view, the goal of social welfare is an obligatory goal of considerable moral force.

Fortunately, there is no need to decide between these two moral perspectives because, as I propose to show, the libertarian perspective, when correctly interpreted, can be seen to require much the same obligatory goal for social welfare that is endorsed by the welfare liberal perspective.[11]

Now the libertarian perspective has been defended in basically two different ways. Some libertarians, following Herbert Spenser, have 1) defined liberty as the absence of constraints, 2) taken a right to liberty to be the ultimate political ideal, and 3) derived all other rights from this right to liberty. Other libertarians, following John Locke, have 1) taken a set of rights, including, typically, a right to life or self-ownership and a right to property, to be the ultimate political ideal, and 2) defined liberty as the absence of constraints in the exercise of these fundamental rights, and 3) derived all other rights, including a right to liberty, from these fundamental rights.

Each of these approaches has its difficulties, but I don't propose to try to decide between them. What I do want to show is that on either approach welfare rights, and, hence, an obligatory goal for social welfare can be morally justified.

Spenserian Libertarianism

Thus suppose we were to adopt the view of those libertarians who take a right to liberty to be the ultimate political ideal. According to this view, liberty is usually defined as follows:

The Want Conception of Liberty: Liberty is being unconstrained by other persons from doing what one wants.

Now this conception limits the scope of liberty in two ways. First, not all constraints whatever their source count as a restriction of liberty; the constraints must come from other persons. For example, people who are constrained by natural forces from getting to the top of Mount Everest do not lack liberty in this regard. Second, constraints that have their source in other persons, but that do not run counter to an individual's wants, constrain without restricting that individual's liberty. Thus, for people who do not want to hear Beethoven's Fifth Symphony, the fact that others have effectively proscribed its performance does not restrict their liberty, even though it does constrain what they are able to do.

Of course, libertarians may wish to argue that even such constraints can be seen to restrict a person's liberty once we take into account the fact that people normally want, or have a general desire, to be unconstrained by others. But other philosophers have thought that the possibility of such constraints points to a serious defect in this conception of liberty,[12] which can only be remedied by adopting the following broader conception of liberty:

> The Ability Conception of Liberty: Liberty is being unconstrained by other persons from doing what one is able to do.

Applying this conception to the above example, we find that people's liberty to hear Beethoven's Fifth Symphony would be restricted even if they did not want to hear it (and even if, perchance, they did not want to be unconstrained by others) since other people would still be constraining them from doing what they are able to do.

Yet even if we accept all the liberties specified by the Ability Conception, problems of interpretation still remain. The major problem in this regard concerns what is to count as a constraint. On the one hand, libertarians would like to limit constraints to positive acts (i.e., acts of commission) that prevent people from doing what they are otherwise able to do. On the other hand, welfare liberals interpret constraints to include, in addition, negative acts (i.e., acts of omission) that prevent people from doing what they are otherwise able to do. In fact, this is one way to understand the debate between defenders of "negative liberty" and defenders of "positive liberty." For defenders of negative liberty would seem to interpret constraints to include only positive acts of others that prevent people from doing what they otherwise are able to do, while defenders of positive liberty would seem to interpret constraints to include both positive and negative acts of others that prevent people from doing what they are otherwise able to do.[13]

Now suppose we interpret constraints in the manner favored by libertarians to include only positive acts by others that prevent people from doing what they are otherwise able to do, and let us consider a typical conflict situation between the rich and the poor.

In this conflict situation, the rich, of course, have more than enough resources to satisfy their basic needs. By contrast, the poor lack the resources to meet their most basic needs even though they have tried all the means available to them in a libertarian society for acquiring such resources. Under circumstances like these, libertarians usually maintain that the rich should have the liberty to use their resources to satisfy their luxury needs if they so wish. Libertarians recognize that this liberty might well be enjoyed at the expense of the satisfaction of the most basic needs of the poor. Libertarians just think that a right to liberty always has priority over other political ideals, and since they assume that the liberty of the poor is not at stake in such conflict situations, it is easy for them to conclude that the rich should not be required to sacrifice their liberty so that the basic needs of the poor may be met.

From a consideration of the liberties involved, libertarians claim to derive a number of more specific requirements, in particular, a right to life, a right to freedom of speech, press and assembly, and a right to property.

Here it is important to observe that the libertarian's right to life is not a right to receive from others the goods and resources necessary for preserving one's life; it is simply a right not to be killed unjustly. Correspondingly, the libertarian's right to property is not a right to receive from others the goods and resources necessary for one's welfare, but rather a right to acquire goods and resources either by initial acquisition or by voluntary agreement.

Of course, libertarians would allow that it would be nice of the rich to share their surplus resources with the poor. Nevertheless, according to libertarians, such acts of charity should not be coercively required, because the liberty of the poor is not thought to be at stake in such conflict situations.

In fact, however, the liberty of the poor is at stake in such conflict situations. What is at stake is the liberty of the poor to take from the surplus possessions of the rich what is necessary to satisfy their basic needs. When libertarians are brought to see that this is the case, they are genuinely surprised, for they had not previously seen the conflict between the rich and the poor as a conflict of liberties.[14]

Now when the conflict between the rich and poor is viewed

as a conflict of liberties, we can either say that the rich should have the liberty to use their surplus resources for luxury purposes, or we can say that the poor should have the liberty to take from the rich what they require to meet their basic needs. If we choose one liberty, we must reject the other. What needs to be determined, therefore, is which liberty is morally preferable: the liberty of the rich or the liberty of the poor.

I submit that the liberty of the poor, which is the liberty to take from the surplus resources of others what is required to meet one's basic needs, is morally preferable to the liberty of the rich, which is the liberty to use one's surplus resources for luxury purposes. To see that this is the case we need only appeal to one of the most fundamental principles of morality, one that is common to all political perspectives, namely, the "ought" implies "can" principle. According to this principle, people are not morally required to do what they lack the power to do or what would involve so great a sacrifice that it would be unreasonable to ask them to perform such an action.[15] Now it seems clear that the poor have it within their power to willingly relinquish such an important liberty as the liberty to take from the rich what they require to meet their basic needs. Yet it would be unreasonable to ask them to make so great a sacrifice. In the extreme case, it would involve asking the poor to sit back and starve to death. Of course, the poor may have no real alternative to relinquishing this liberty. To do anything else may involve worse consequences for themselves and their loved ones and may invite a painful death. Accordingly, we may expect that the poor would acquiesce, albeit unwillingly, to a political system that denied them the welfare rights supported by such a liberty, at the same time that we recognize that such a system imposes an unreasonable sacrifice upon the poor--a sacrifice that we could not morally blame the poor for trying to evade.[16] Analogously, we might expect that a woman whose life was threatened would submit to a rapist's demands, at the same time that we recognize the utter unreasonableness of those demands.

By contrast, it would not be unreasonable to ask the rich to sacrifice the liberty to meet some of their luxury needs so that the poor can have the liberty to meet their basic needs. Of course, we might expect that the rich for reasons of self-interest might be disinclined to make such a sacrifice. Yet, unlike the poor, the rich could not claim that relinquishing such a liberty involved so great a sacrifice that it would be unreasonable to ask them to make it; unlike the poor, the rich could be morally blameworthy for failing to make such a sacrifice.

Consequently, if we assume that however else we specify the requirements of morality, they cannot violate the "ought" implies "can" principle, it follows that, despite what libertarians claim, the right to liberty endorsed by libertarians actually favors the liberty of the poor over the liberty of the rich.

Yet couldn't libertarians object to this conclusion, claiming that it would be unreasonable to ask the rich to sacrifice the liberty to meet some of their luxury needs so that the poor could have the liberty to meet their basic needs? As I have pointed out, libertarians don't usually see the situations as a conflict of liberties, but suppose they did. How plausible would such an objection be? Not very plausible at all, I think.

For consider: what are libertarians going to say about the poor? Isn't it clearly unreasonable to ask the poor to sacrifice the liberty to meet their basic needs so that the rich can have the liberty to meet their luxury needs? Isn't it clearly unreasonable to ask the poor to sit back and starve to death? If it is, then there is no resolution of this conflict that would be reasonable to ask both the rich and the poor to accept. But that would mean that the libertarian ideal of liberty cannot be a moral ideal; for a moral ideal resolves conflicts of interest in ways that it would be reasonable to ask everyone affected to accept. As long as libertarians think of themselves as putting forth a moral ideal, therefore, they cannot allow that it would be unreasonable <u>both</u> to ask the rich to sacrifice the liberty to meet some of their luxury needs in order to benefit the poor and to ask the poor to sacrifice the liberty to meet their basic needs in order to benefit the rich. But I submit that if one of these requests is to be judged reasonable, then, by any neutral assessment, it must be the request that the rich sacrifice the liberty to meet some of their luxury needs so that the poor can have the liberty to meet their basic needs; there is no other plausible resolution, if libertarians intend to be putting forth a moral ideal.

Lockean Libertarianism

Yet suppose we were to adopt the view of those libertarians who do not take a right to liberty to be the ultimate political ideal. According to this view, liberty is defined as follows:

<u>The Rights Conception of Liberty</u>: Liberty is being constrained by other persons from doing what one has a right to do.

And the most important ultimate rights in terms of which liberty is specified are, according to this view, a right to life understood as a right not to be killed unjustly and a right to property understood as a right to acquire goods and resources either by initial acquisition or voluntary agreement. Now in order to evaluate this view, we must determine what are the practical implications of these rights.

Presumably, a right to life understood as a right not to be killed unjustly would not be violated by defensive measures designed to protect one's person from life-threatening attacks. Yet would this right be violated when the rich prevent the poor from taking what they require to satisfy their basic needs? Obviously, as a consequence of such preventive actions poor people sometimes do starve to death. Have the rich, then, in contributing to this result, killed the poor, or simply let them die; and, if they have killed the poor, have they done so unjustly?

Now sometimes the rich in preventing the poor from taking what they require to meet their basic needs would not in fact be killing the poor, but only causing them to be physically or mentally debilitated. Yet since such preventive acts involve resisting the life-preserving activities of the poor, when the poor do die as a consequences of such acts, it seems clear that the rich would be killing the poor, whether intentionally or unintentionally.

Of course, libertarians would want to argue that such killing is simply a consequence of the legitimate exercise of property rights, and hence, not unjust. But to understand why libertarians are mistaken in this regard, let us appeal again to that fundamental principle of morality, the "ought" implies "can" principle. In this context, the principle can be used to assess two opposing accounts of property rights. According to the first account, a right to property is <u>not</u> conditional upon whether other persons have sufficient opportunities and resources to satisfy their basic needs. This view holds that the initial acquisition and voluntary agreement of some can leave others, through no fault of their own, dependent upon charity for the satisfaction of their most basic needs. By contrast, according to the second account, initial acquisition and voluntary agreement can confer title of property on all goods and resources except those surplus goods and resources of the rich that are required to satisfy the basic needs of those poor who through no fault of their own lack the opportunities and resources to satisfy their own basic needs.

Clearly, only the first of these two accounts of property rights would generally justify the killing of the poor as a legitimate exercise of the property rights of the rich. Yet it would be unreasonable to ask the poor to accept anything other than some version of the second account of property rights. Moreover, according to the second account, it does not matter whether the poor would actually die or are only physically or mentally debilitated as a result of such acts of prevention. Either result would preclude property rights from arising. Of course, the poor may have no real alternative to acquiescing to a political system modeled after the first account of property rights, even though such a system imposes an unreasonable sacrifice upon them--a sacrifice that we could not blame them for trying to evade. At the same time, although the rich would be disinclined to do so, it would not be unreasonable to ask them to accept a political system modeled after the second account or property rights--the account favored by the poor.

Consequently, if we assume that however else we specify the requirements of morality, they cannot violate the "ought" implies "can" principle, it follows that despite what libertarians claim, the right to life and the right to property required by their ideal actually support a system of welfare rights. This means that whether one endorses a libertarian perspective or a welfare liberal perspective much the same obligatory goal for social welfare will be required.

The Priority Question

Having tentatively established what are the legitimate goals of national defense and social welfare, we are now in a position to raise the question of whether one of these goals has priority over the other. This is a difficult question. Fortunately, in most cases the question need not be faced because both goals can be adequately met. Moreover, in such circumstances meeting both goals would seem to be morally required. This means that if a nation must spend more to satisfy the goal of national defense, the tax burden for meeting this goal must fall on its wealthier citizens and not jeopardize at all the welfare rights of the poor. Judged in these terms, the present U.S. policy of cutting back on non-entitlement social welfare programs in order to pave the way for a build-up of U.S. military forces cannot be morally justified. In addition, if a particular nation cannot satisfy the goal of national defense without denying basic welfare to some of its citizens, that nation if possible must work out a cost-sharing plan with its allies so as not to deprive its citizens of their basic welfare.

But suppose the two goals cannot be jointly satisfied. What then? In this quite unusual situation it would appear that the goal of national defense would have priority over the goal of social welfare. The reason for this is, first of all, that meeting the goal of national defense is a fundamental need for the members of a society, and, secondly, that the goal of social welfare depends for its legitimate satisfaction on the availability of a surplus after the fundamental needs of the members of a society have been satisfied. And so in the unlikely eventuality that no surplus existed except what is necessary to meet the goal of national defense, the goal of social welfare would have to be sacrificed.

In sum, then, I have argued _first_ that the legitimate goal of national defense would interpret optimal military security so that it requires some version of alternatives (4) or (5) and, _second_ that the legitimate goal of social welfare is an obligatory requirement that we meet the basic needs of the poor and _third_ that in normal circumstances both goals must be met so that only rarely would a nation be justified in sacrificing the goal of social welfare to the goal of national defense.

University of Notre Dame

NOTES

1. These figures are derived from the *Economic Report of the President 1984,* Washington, D.C.: U.S. Government Printing Office, p. 305ff.

2. Caspar W. Weinberger, *Annual Report to the Congress Fiscal Year 1984,* Washington, D.C.: U.S. Government Printing Office.

3. Gregory Kavka, "Nuclear Deterrence: Some Moral Perplexities" in *The Ethics of War and Nuclear Deterrence* edited by James P. Sterba, Belmont: Wadsworth Publishing Co., 1984.

4. Gregory Kavka, "The Paradoxes of Deterrence" in *The Journal of Philosophy* (1978).

5. Michael Walzer, "Nuclear Deterrence" in *Morality in Practice* edited by James P. Sterba, Belmont: Wadsworth Publishing Co., 1983, pp. 315-323.

6. *Ibid.,* p. 318.

7. Jonathan Schell, "The Contradiction of Nuclear Deterrence" in *Morality in Practice,* pp. 324-330.

8. *Ibid.,* p. 325.

9. Alternatively, Gregory Kavka has suggested that the leaders of a nation might make themselves into immoral agents who would be willing to carry out an immoral use of nuclear weapons should deterrence fail (see his "The Paradoxes of Deterrence"). This would be, in effect, an attempt to get deterrence by creating a "human doomsday machine." But his alternative, like that of achieving deterrence by bluffing, is not required to achieve the desired degree of deterrence. In addition, once a nation's leaders succeeded in making themselves into immoral agents, it would be difficult to limit their immoral actions to simply threatening an immoral use of nuclear weapons.

10. James P. Sterba, "How to Achieve Nuclear Deterrence without Threatening Nuclear Destruction," in *The Ethics of War and Nuclear Deterrence.*

11. I issued a promissory note to this effect at the Bowling Green Conference on Social Justice held two years ago. (See James P. Sterba, "Some Problems With 'Making Justice Practical'," *Social Justice* edited by David Braybrooke and Michael Bradie (Bowling Green, 1982), pp. 18-19.)

12. Isaiah Berlin, *Four Essays on Liberty* (New York, 1969), pp. xxxviii-xi.

13. F.A. Hayek, *The Construction of Liberty* (Chicago, 1960), p. 18. On this point, see Maurice Cranston, *Freedom* (New York, 1953), pp. 52-53; C.B. Macpherson, *Democratic Theory* (Oxford, 1973), pp. 95-97; Joel Feinberg, *Rights, Justice and the Bounds of Liberty* (Princeton, 1980), Chapter 1.

14. See John Hospers, *Libertarianism* (Los Angeles, 1971), Chapter 7.

15. Alvin Goldman, *A Theory of Human Action* (Englewood Cliffs, 1970), pp. 208-215; William Frankena, "Obligation and Ability" in *Philosophical Analysis* edited by Max Black (Ithaca, 1950), pp. 157-175. Judging from some recent discussions of moral dilemmas by Bernard Williams and Ruth Marcus, one might think that the "ought" implies "can" principle would only be useful for illustrating moral conflicts rather than resolving them. (See Bernard Williams, *Problem of the Self* (1977), Chapters 11 and 12; Ruth Marcus, "Moral Dilemmas and Consistency" in *The Journal of Philosophy* (1980), pp. 121-136. See also Terrance C. McConnell, "Moral Dilemmas and Consistency in Ethics" in *Canadian Journal of Philosophy* (1978), pp. 269-287, but this is only true if one interprets the "can" in the principle to exclude only "what a person lacks the power to do." If one interprets the "can" to exclude in addition "what would involve so great a sacrifice that it would be unreasonable to ask the person to do

it" then the principle can be used to resolve moral conflicts as well as state them. Nor would libertarians object to this broader interpretation of the "ought" implies "can" principle since they do not ground their claim to liberty on the existence of irresolvable moral conflicts.

16. See my paper, "Is There a Rationale for Punishment" in *the Americal Journal of Jurisprudence* (1984).

DISPLACED WORKERS: WHOSE RESPONSIBILITY?[1]

Edmund F. Byrne

When America was a young nation it was easier to believe that the frontier really represented opportunity for those who were willing to work. The frontier, however, is forever gone; and willingness to work is no longer any assurance of opportunity. For, while there is certainly no shortage of tasks to perform, performance that is remunerated in our capitalist economy depends primarily on jobs; and there just are not enough jobs to go around. Experts debate why this is so and whether anything can be done about it. But while the debate goes on, a veritable revolution in the processes of performance is rapidly diminishing the need, once thought so great, for people willing to work. Microelectronic devices, such as robots and word processors, are picking up where scientific management left off; and the humans they are displacing carry the stamp of obsolescence on their badges.[2]

Enter at this cue an old metaphysical concern about whether technology is neutral or perhaps something more value-laden in our regard. In this instance, however, as in perhaps very few others, the metaphysics of it all is too serious to leave to the metaphysicians. Labor unions in particular have had to deal with this question, at least implicitly. In Europe they do so explicitly; and for reasons ideological as well as tactical, they tend to favor the neutralist position, saving their energy to do battle against a coterie of unintended consequences. This is the case, for example, in France, where Marxism is the ideology of preference within the union hierarchy.[3] In the United Kingdom, on the other hand, Marxist laborites are on the fringes of power and tend to take the position that those in control of the unions are at fault precisely because they do accept technology as neutral and hence do not fight with sufficient vigor against it.[4]

On the basis of this assumption of neutrality, unions in Europe and Japan as well as the UAW and the CWA in the United States have sought "data agreements" and "new technology agreements" as ways of mitigating the impact of robots, word processors and such on the jobs of those presently doing what these devices have been designed to do better. These agreements do on occasion provide substantial benefits to workers displaced by new technology. But they are just as likely to settle for some tangential benefit such as a limitation on the number of hours a day an employee can be required to work in front of a visual display unit. Moreover, the vast majority of these agreements, at least in Europe and the United States, affect primarily white collar workers, e.g., the members of APEX in the United Kingdom. There is as yet no such agreement at any national, not to mention international, level. Rather are these agreements usually at plant or on occasion company level; and they are seldom arrived at without considerable resistance on the part of management.[5]

In addition to bargained agreements that ameliorate somewhat the impact of new technology on workers, some progress has been made through legislation and, to a lesser extent, through litigation. At issue here is the emerging claim of unfair dismissal or, as it is sometimes called, abusive discharge. Some workers have a statutory cause of action if dismissed in retaliation for having exercised rights granted under the statute in question. Others, mostly managerial or professional, have achieved comparable results through judicial rethinking of traditional concepts of law especially with regard to contracts. The overall effect to date has been a narrowing of the scope of a nineteenth century laissez-faire device known as "employment at will" (EAW, hereafter), which suggests that a mythical mutuality of contract implies the right of either party to end the relationship without cause.[6]

In reality, these modifications are minimally responsive to the social and economic problems that worker displacement is already imposing upon our outmoded laissez-faire public policy with regard to work and the lack of work. Considering the scope of technological unemployment that we face in most occupations and up and down the hierarchy of the work force, mere "sauve qui peut" stopgap measures are inadequate. Jobs are not merely being moved from one place to another, from East to West or from North to South or even from home to abroad, as has historically been the case. Jobs are being taken from humans and given to presumably more efficient, reliable and productive machines, in particular those that are driven microelectronically. Workers thus replaced may, as in the case of Western Electric employees being phased out over the next several years, be provided with a better than customary "transitional" cushion.[7] But in many such instances no new job is likely to be forthcoming.

In a word, we as a society need to decide who should assume what responsibility for the societal transition that is already underway. What follows is intended as a contribution to the discussion of this question of responsibility in the form of a series of arguments, none of which is particularly original. ("L" stands loosely for Labor; "C," for Capital.)

L1. Exploitation of Workers. Management is to blame for the current work place crisis because of its long history of manipulating people into servile dependence by touting the work ethic on the one hand and EAW on the other. The unprincipled ruthlessness that underlies this two-pronged manipulation of workers is evident in management's simultaneous efforts over the years to achieve productivity without payrolls. First they Taylorized brains out of jobs as much as possible, then they started looking for and introducing machines to do the brainless jobs. Now, to their surprise, they have at their disposal even brainier machines that will allow them (those who are left) to shrink the payroll even more by eliminating even personnel recognized as having some brains.

C1. Advantages of EAW to Employees. In the course of the twentieth century, the alleged severity of EAW has been tempered in a variety of ways, as a result of legislation, regulation, and especially contract bargaining with regard to the terms and conditions of employment. This tempering has improved the status of the employee and of both the potential and the former employee. And the other side of the coin, don't forget, is the freedom of the employee to quit the job in question and take skills, often employer-taught, to a better job with another employer. To prohibit such mobility is to require involuntary servitude, which is prohibited in all of the civilized world, including the United States since the Civil War.

L2. Disadvantages of EAW to Employees. As a matter of fact, there are still employees in the United States, especially in agriculture, who have been maneuvered by their employers into positions of involuntary servitude. Leaving this problem aside, it is unrealistic to equate the freedom of the employee to end a work relationship with that of the employer. Such an equation may apply in the case of the small proprietary business. But another order of magnitude is involved in the case of a large corporation that has located a plant in a particular community under certain terms and conditions over an extended period of time. This large corporate employer may well have become the only ongoing source of income for its employees and for others economically dependent on them. To justify that kind of employer's dismissal of, typically, thousands of employees on the basis of EAW is comparable to appealing to self-defense to justify grand larceny.

The basic presupposition of this doctrine, namely, the mutuality (i.e., equal bargaining position) of the parties, has not been seriously undermined. Regardless of developments abroad, e.g., in Sweden, not even the most powerful unions in the United States have been able to prevent plant closings and massive layoffs. Improved provisions for the time of "transition" do not change the basic fact that large corporate employers can and do end one-to-many relationships with consequences quite devastating outside the four corners of their ledger sheets.

C2. The Profit Motive. Problems do arise when an employer is required by business necessity to reduce a work force, close a plant, cut back on production of a product or even shut down completely. But when profitability is insufficient, there is no alternative that is or should be acceptable to investors, including, as often as not, the pension funds of many, even millions of, workers.

Besides, you can hardly blame management for a philosophy of work with which even unions have agreed to a great extent, at least with regard to the idea that the work relationship is dependent upon the availability of work as determined by management. In any event, it is essential to a free enterprise system that an employer not be required to pay someone as an employee regardless of the profitability of the employment in question. Cost-cutting, including plant relocation and work force reduction, must always be available as options if we are to attract the capital that makes employment possible.

L3. Bad Management. An employer should in principle have the right to be free of an unproductive worker (and/or machine or plant or division), but only on condition that he/she (it) is in no way <u>responsible</u> for that worker's lack of productivity. In particular, persons (employees) have rights not granted to mere equipment. If the failure of my watch to "work" any more is due entirely to my own negligence, e.g., having worn it into the swimming pool knowing it not to be waterproof, I still retain the right to dispose of it without pausing to contemplate its future. I do, however, <u>own</u> another person as I might own a watch by virtue of my <u>being</u> that person's employer. So to the extent that I am responsible for that person's becoming less productive or unproductive, I continue to have obligations vis-a-vis that person. If I failed to provide tools and equipment in a timely way, if I failed to seek customers (e.g., as a contractor), if I failed to modernize to stay competitive in my business environment (e.g., as in the case of West German watchmaking or U.S. steel production), if I failed to manage prudently,[8] then am I not for any of these reasons responsible for the financial/social misfortune of the person who has come to work for me? The other side of "management rights," in other words, is management responsibility. Claim the one and you must accept the other, as some judges are now finding when they consider the terms of the employment contract. To say otherwise is to raise the crassest kind of exploitation to the level of public policy.

<u>C3. Risk Control</u>. A negligent employer may indeed be held responsible for <u>some</u> misfortunes of an employee, e.g., with regard to the employee's health and safety on the job. Hence the need for appropriate insurance and, maybe, some form of governmental oversight. Such responsibility must be circumscribed, however, or the employer will remain forever uncertain of its financial status. Take away these limits on an employer's responsibility, expose the employer to open-ended liability, and you create a monster that will devour management and labor in one big bite. Witness the numerous business failures in recent years; management is no less at risk in the face of technological change than are workers. So if business is to be encouraged to the benefit of all concerned it ought not to be exposed unduly to interference on the part of courts with regard to terms of employment. Leave that to the parties immediately involved, either one-on-one or by means of

collective bargaining, to come to terms understood and acceptable on both sides.

L4. Unequal Parties. Contrary to the traditional mythology still canonized by most courts, contracting parties in the employment situation are seldom bargaining at arm's length. The typical work relationship today is between comparatively vulnerable workers and a large corporation. It is accordingly quite appropriate for society, through its courts and otherwise, to base its work policies on the realities of the working world today rather than on the alleged need for entrepreneurial autonomy that characterized the pioneering days of the nineteenth century. There is precedent for just this sort of rethinking the realities in the recent U.S. Supreme Court decision in Container Corp. of America vs. [California] Franchise Tax Board, which frees states to develop tax formulas that take into account the global profits of a corporation operating within its borders.[9]

C4. Union Power. The heavily one-sided employment relationship just described is more typical of the previous century than it is today. In the interim the labor movement has organized much of the work place, thereby giving workers power equal to that of the management. And even if the majority of workers, at least in the United States, are not organized, the legal structures are there to make such organization available to them if they feel a need to bargain with their employer collectively, especially concerning job security.

L5. Constraints on Unions. The previous argument must be tongue-in-cheek in view of management's dedicated efforts over the years to see to it that as small a percentage as possible of workers organize. In particular, it conveniently disregards all the legal constraints that have been imposed on union organizing since the end of World War II. Anti-union statutes such as the Labor Management Relations Act of 1947 (Taft-Hartley) and the Labor Management Reporting and Disclosure Act of 1959 (Landrum-Griffin), as well as anti-union interpretations of statutes, e.g., concerning antitrust and, more recently, bankruptcy laws, severely hamper the growth of unions in the United States.[10] In 1978, labor efforts to have Congress put teeth into the statutory prohibition of employer obstruction of organizing met with heavy and ultimately successful opposition from business interests. Thus even an umbrella organization such as the AFL-CIO can do little in the face of plant closings, outsourceing, change of product and/or process (automation). These law-embodied constraints on the labor movement represent as much as anything else in our society what is in fact our society's policy with regard to the rights of workers in the face of corporate changes that cost jobs and, in many instances, undermine the economies of entire communities. So it is rather hypocritical to appeal now to the right to organize as an answer to technological unemployment.

C5. Democratic Process. The position of unions in the United States has deteriorated in recent years because of the competition-engendered decline of the most highly organized industries. But this deterioration is neither inevitable nor irremediable. If we as a society so choose, we can still change our public policy with regard to job security, as has been done in Sweden, or our approach to industrial policy below the level of government, as has been done in Japan, West Germany, and the United Kingdom. We as a people need only be persuaded that it is in our long-term best interest to be more solicitous of workers necessarily left by the wayside as we move on to new technologies. As evidence of this, consider how EAW has been modified over the years to accommodate the legitimate demands of employees who challenge their dismissal.

L6. Power of MNC's. Nation-states themselves, even one as powerful as the United States of America, are inadequate instruments of effective industrial policy in this age of massive multinational corporations (MNC's, hereafter), some of which have annual budgets larger than those of most national governments combined. Salvador Allende (and his British industrial policy adviser, Stafford Beer) learned this harsh lesson at the hands of U.S.-based corporate enterprise, whose views were subsequently expressed in Chile by conservative economist Milton Friedman.[11] Others, such as Simon Nora in his report to the President of France Giscard d'Estaing, also see what the United States Supreme Court has now seen, that the MNC can shift its assets and liabilities around by paper (or, rather, microelectronic) transfers that most effectively immunize the company's proceeds. Neither our government nor any other is capable by itself of formulating a policy that will effectively solve the problem of technological unemployment.

C6. International Law. Pessimism is not a justification for inactivity. Even granting the seriousness of these complaints about the impotence of nation-states in the age of the MNC, one is reminded all the more forcefully of the need for a world government that is capable of rising beyond the provincial limits of the past. This sort of supra-national structure already exists in limited form in such world-oriented agencies as the United Nations and its subsidiaries, such as the WHO and the FEO, and the IMF, the EEC, GATT, and various other structures developed under the principles of international law. These international arrangements are admittedly inadequate; but by their very existence they attest to the possibility of building broader-based agencies necessary to the survival and advancement of the human family.

L7. Corporate Responsibility. World government, even if possible, may not be desirable. But the question is moot, since no world government presently exists. Even if there were a world government, empowered to determine somehow the rights of workers around the world, it would need some basis on which to make such an important determination. The establishment of this basis for determination of rights should precede any actual set of laws in any particular governmental unit, however advanced. What is needed for this purpose, however, is an emerging sense of human rights with regard to work prior to and independently of any particular politico-economic arrangements, be they in a developed or a developing country. The most widely honored statement of human rights, however, namely, the Declaration of Human Rights, speaks only of the right to work, not of any rights in the absence of available work. And merely expanding the traditional notion of a work ethic beyond national borders is hardly an adequate way to deal with a problem that is brought on precisely by the diminishing availability of economically rewardable work. So leave world-building to a future generation. There are issues enough before us just with regard to the legal environment of work in particular locales, such as the United States. Here there are good reasons for laying responsibility for technological unemployment at management's door.

C7. Social Responsibility. There is almost always a simple solution to every problem; but, unfortunately, it is almost always wrong. If you want to make the employer responsible for technological unemployment, then what you mean is that you want the public, via higher prices for the employer's products, to pay for the employee's historically inevitable misfortune. To every action there is an equal and opposite reaction. In the context of systems thinking, this comes down to saying that you can't do just one thing. A system by definition is a set of components so interrelated that a change in one effects changes in all. With this in mind, there is a need today to develop a global system the components of which are known, anticipated, and taken into account in planning for the future so as to keep the shifting MNC under control. So be it. But this cannot be achieved overnight. In the meantime, employers, wherever based, must compete in the world marketplace.

In the case of American-based companies, however responsible they may have been historically for the policies that worked well enough within our national borders, they did not formulate those policies in a vacuum. Government (whether responsibly or not is beside the point) went along with, even canonized those policies, which served us all well enough through the years of nation building. If a new consensus is in fact required for the coming era of world building, then let us get on with it. But let us do so not in an adversarial relationship of "the people" against "business." Let us rather recognize the universal myopia that characterized our past even as we were building a base for our future. And having acknowledged this myopia for what it was, let us now, as a society, take collective responsibility for the victims of our shortsightedness. And for this project we might well accept as a basic maxim that any group or institution should be held responsible, or liable, for worker displacement no more or less than it has been involved in the decision-making that has led to the present crisis.

L8. Corporate Bias. This plea for diffusing responsibility beyond corporate headquarters under the guise of "collective responsibility" has the support of history inasmuch as corporate decision-making has over the years enjoyed benign neglect at the hands of government in the United States, e.g., with regard to plant closings. And some would have it so now and forever. In particular, it is now being contended that "foreign competition" requires leaving business even more unhampered than before so that it can find new and better ways of competing, e.g., by the introduction of robots. What is left off this agenda, however, is any consideration of the scope of interests that will in fact be served by such flexibility. Business left to itself will consider only the interests of its investors, not those of its workers. So if workers cannot protect themselves on their own, e.g., by winning some guarantee of job security, then government ought to help them. For after all, if there are great benefits allegedly to be derived from displacing workers, then why not let some of those benefits redound to the workers being asked to sacrifice themselves to that end?

C8. Worker Control. If the cause of concern here is management's inability to represent workers fairly and objectively in these crisis situations, this can be remedied by expanding the role of workers in decision-making, not only on the shop floor but on executive boards as well. To the shared responsibility of management and workers on a board of directors can also be added appropriate governmental input. The broader the representation, the better the input and the better the resulting output in the form of policy. In this way, management would retain responsibility but would share it with representatives of both workers and government. Quality circles, profit-sharing plans, ESOP's, worker ownership, and various other arrangements, as appropriate, can be utilized to increase worker involvement in and appreciation of challenges to the survival and growth of the company by which they are employed. With some modification of the legal constraints on unions, referred to above, unions could even take responsibility for some of these new approaches to management, so long as they would not thereby enter into unfair competition in the very industry one is trying to salvage.[12]

L9. Economic Policy Planning.[13] Even management can sound pro-labor if the situation is desperate enough. Worker ownership is a good example. How often do you hear of employees being offered ownership of a thriving business? Rather, employees are turned to as a convenient way to bail out of a plant or business with minimum damage to the corporate image before community and customers. The ultimate proponent of this ploy may even turn out to be the Reagan

Administration as it looks for a way to get Conrail (Consolidated Rail Corp.) off the public ledger.[14] As this example illustrates, deregulation is about as close as the U.S. government has come to any coordinated, consistent industrial plan. The marketplace is even being counted on, it seems, to assure this country a supply of oil in the event of another cut-off. But not even an economy as large as that of the United States can function effectively in the face of world competition without serious broad-based planning combined with research and development. Nor can we rely any more on incidental civilian applications of military R&D.[15] The Japanese, among others, study world markets on a national level, locate areas of business decline, stagnation, and growth, then focus R&D accordingly. Companies collaborate on R&D (no need for domestic industrial spying) and do their competing with products in the marketplace.[16] Similarly, the West German government controls industrial plant relocation by assessing the total cost of any proposed move, including the cost to workers, on the infrastructure.[17]

By comparison, America's industrial policy is practically non-existent, to the point that the out-of-power Democrats would have a claim on the White House if only they could come up with such a policy after years of relying in vain on fiscal manipulation.[18] Instead, Washington deregulates, talks about local content for products to be consumed domestically, and peddles a strong dollar that puts export-dependent jobs in mothballs. There is even some reason to fear that our government is counting on a Depression-generated idea that even in a nuclear age war can cure economic woes, including unemployment. Hopefully, costs and benefits of such an approach will be assessed fully enough to show forth its obviously fatal fallacy. But such brinkmanship thinking does suggest the need for more than merely a band-aid approach to curing unemployment.

Band-aids are needed, as are tourniquets and even transfusions. But beyond all this there is need for us to go beyond concern just for the transition of the worker (adequate, if at all, only for cyclical, or frictional, unemployment) to concern about moving from an obsolete industrial base to one with a very different mix of skill requirements and resulting employment needs.[19]

C9. Growth through Autonomy. Disregarding the rhetorical excess of the preceding statement, it is unobjectionable except for its implicit assumption that government can solve any problem through the magic of its burdensome bureaucracy. Anyone who believes this needs to explain why welfare programs developed in West European countries in decades past are being cut back by survival-bent governments at both ends of the political spectrum.[20] As companies such as Peoplexpress are proving, deregulation of an industry can lead to many jobs with a provider of affordable goods or services. Granted there is need for better planning. Any business that has to meet the competition knows very well indeed that profitability, not to mention survival, depends upon a well laid out plan of attack on the market. So why ask government to do at great cost what competition does for free?

So much for arguments in behalf of Labor and Capital regarding responsibility for displaced workers. The winner is hardly apparent. But Labor does have strong evidence for a claim that it is being treated very badly in this country; and random judicial victories over EAW will not suffice to balance the scales of justice. On the other hand, random expansion of workers' defenses against EAW would unduly hamper management's ability to meet unquestionably serious competition from abroad. But we are all of us losers if we as a nation continue to abandon displaced workers like tools no longer needed. We do not cut off benefits to veterans of yesterday's wars just because they served with now obsolete means of destruction. Still less should workers be forgotten simply because they served with now obsolete means of production. Yet full employment however defined is probably an unattainable goal at least for the foreseeable future. What, then, is to be done and how ought we to do it?

For one thing, we should be developing a national work policy that would in effect expand considerably the scope of protective legislation. For, at the very time we are being urged to start planning for leisure on a massive scale,[21] those who are employed are likely to be working inordinate overtime hours or at a second job. So there is already a need to distribute available work more rationally and equitably; and this could be accomplished, at least in part, through a combination of laws setting a minimum level of income and a maximum level of hours of employment (without regard to self-created jobs). Additional steps into the age of leisure should include not just a new national holiday every decade or so, but an orderly plan for distributing reduced manpower needs by means of shorter work weeks, longer vacations (as in Western Europe) and even "sabbaticals" for all workers. Whatever our approach to the declining need for work in our society, we have an excellent opportunity to reconsider what, after all, we really value in our lives. For, workers of the previous generation, whatever they may have contributed to society, are now at the mercy of their progeny. Hopefully, the latter will find a way to pay their forebears the debt they clearly owe.

Indiana University

NOTES

1. Based on an article entitled "Displaced Workers: America's Unpaid Debt," copyright 1985 by D. Reidel Publishing Company, Dordrecht, Holland.

2. See Edmund F. Byrne, "Robots and the Future of Work," in *The World of Work: Careers and the Future,* ed. Howard F. Didsbury, Jr., Bethesda, Md.: World Future Society, 1983, pp. 30-38.

3. Personal communication, Daniel Cerezuelle, University of Bourdeaux, Bourdeaux, France.

4. Ian Benson and John Lloyd, *New Technology and Industrial Change: The Impact of the Scientific-Technical Revolution on Labour and Industry,* London: Kegan Paul, 1983, pp. 165-84.

5. Edmund F. Byrne, "Microelectronics and Workers' Rights," in *Boston Studies in the Philosophy of Science,* ed. Carl Mitcham, forthcoming.

6. Gary E. Murg and Clifford Scharman, "Employment at Will: Do the Exceptions Overwhelm the Rule?" *Boston College L. Rev.* 23 (March 1982) pp. 329-330, nn. 1-2; pp. 337, nn. 48-50.

7. *The Indianapolis Star,* Sept. 12-16, 1983, *passim.*

8. See "Shortcomings of Management," in *More Construction for the Money: Summary Report of the Construction Industry Cost Effectiveness Project,* New York: The Business Roundtable, 1983, pp. 21-30. Compare "Union Workers May Really Be More Productive," *Business Week,* Aug. 22, 1983, p. 22; Charles Brown and James Medoff, "Trade Unions in the Production Process," *Journal of Political Economy* 86 (1978) pp. 355-378; William F. Maloney, "Productivity Bargaining in Contract Construction," 1977 *Labor L.J.,* pp. 532-538.

9. "Now States Can Really Put the Bite on Business," *Business Week,* July 11, 1983.

10. See Deborah Groban Olson, "Union Experiences with Worker Ownership: Legal and Practical Issues Raised by ESOP's, TRASOP's, Stock Purchases and Co-Operatives," 1982 *Wisconsin L. Rev.*, pp. 732-823; Zachary D. Fasman, "Legal Obstacles to Alternative Work Force Designs," 8 *Employee Rel. L.J.* (1982) PP. 256-281; "Worker Ownership and Section 8(a)(2) of the National Labor Relations Act," *Yale L.J.* 91 (1982) pp. 615-33; Harold J. Krent, "Collective Authority and Technical Expertise: Reexamining the Managerial Employee Exclusion," *New York University L. Rev.* 56 (1981) pp. 694-741; Jan Stiglitz, "Union Representation in Construction: Who Makes the Choice?" *San Diego L. Rev.* 18 (1981) pp. 583-632; Lizanne Thomas, "Predatory Intent is an Essential Element of a Union's Antitrust Violation," *Washington and Lee L. Rev.* 38 (1981) pp. 450-459; "Determining Breach of Fiduciary Duty under the Labor-Management Reporting and Disclosure Act: *Gabauer v. Woodcock*," *Harvard L. Rev.* 93 (1980) pp. 608-617; Baker A. Smith, "Landrum-Griffin after Twenty-One Years: Mature Legislation or Childish Fantasy?" 1980 *Labor L.J.* pp. 273-281; Barry A. Macey, "Does Employer Implementation of Employee Production Teams Violate Section 8(a)(2) of the National Labor Relations Act?" *Indiana L.J.* 49 (1974) pp. 516-537; "New Standards for Domination and Support under Section 8(a)(2)," *Yale L.J.* 82 (1973) pp. 510-532; Ralph K. Winter, Jr., "Collective Bargaining and Competition: The Application of Antitrust Standards to Union Activities," *Yale L.J.* 73 (1963) p. 14.

11. Benson and Lloyd, *op. cit.*, p. 200; Andrew Levinson, *The Full Employment Alternative*, New York: Coward, McCann & Geoghegan, 1980, pp. 66-67.

12. See above, n. 10, especially Fasman, *op. cit.*, and Olson, *op. cit.*

13. This expression is taken from Levison, *op. cit.*, pp. 159, 204.

14. "Conrail's Workers Get a Powerful New Ally," *Business Week*, May 14, 1984, p. 157; "The Unions Balk at a Quick Sale of Conrail," *Business Week*, Feb. 27, 1984; "On Track for Conrail: Union Ownership," *Business Week*, June 20, 1983, p. 184. See also *ibid.*, p. 194; April 5, 1982, pp. 72-79; and testimony of Thomas A. Till, Deputy Administrator, Federal Railroad Administration, before U.S. Senate Finance Committee, April 13, 1983.

15. Levison, *op. cit.*, pp. 134-135.

16. Benson and Lloyd, *op. cit.*, pp. 124-127; Ira C. Magaziner and Robert B. Reich, *Minding America's Business*, New York: Vintage, 1983, pp. 261-327. At this writing, it should be noted, there are a number of bills before the 98th U.S. Congress, 1st session, that would modify century-old antitrust law to permit companies to enter into joint ventures for purposes of R&D without exposing themselves to treble damages for restraint of trade. On July 12, 1983, the House Committee on Science and Technology began hearings on H.R. 1952 and H.R. 3393, also assigned to the House Judiciary Committee. Other bills include Democrat-sponsored S.B. 1383 and its counterpart H.B. 108, also S.B. 568, p. 737, and 1561.

17. Levison, *op. cit.*, pp. 110-111.

18. *Ibid.*, pp. 207-209.

19. Magaziner and Reich, *op. cit.*, pp. 210-215. See Levison, *op. cit.*, pp. 83-87, regarding impact of mechanization on workforce in industries such as meat-packing after World War II.

20. "A Risky Operation in the Bloated Welfare State," *Business Week*, Oct. 17, 1983, pp. 56-57.

21. See Clive Jenkins and Barrie Sherman, *The Leisure Shock*, London: Eyre Methuen, 1981; Robert Theobald, "Toward Full Unemployment," in *The World of Work, op. cit.*, pp. 49-58.

FULL EMPLOYMENT:
THE SUPREME ECONOMIC PRIORITY

Jan Narveson

The subject for this session of the conference[1] is "National Economic Priorities." This can, however, be understood in two ways. One way, which would make it analogous to what most of us would mean in our personal lives, would be to interpret it as a call for thought on the main things we should spend our money on. You and I would think, no doubt, of houses, childrens' educations, vacations, investments, hobbies, and so on. But in the case of governments, everything they do costs money, and it would seem that understanding our subject this way would make the expression "economic priorities" equivalent, simply, to "priorities." That presumably is not what is intended.

The other way to interpret it would focus on what is somewhat vaguely described as "economic policy." These are the policies aimed specifically at maintaining, promoting, or perhaps restoring what we might call "economic health," the good functioning of the nation's economy or economic life. That is how I shall construe it in this presentation. So viewed, however, there is the problem that perhaps everything to be done here is really to be done by economists rather than philosophers. This might be understood, in other words, as a subject exclusively for technical expertise in a specialized field of the social sciences. But fortunately for this symposium, it isn't so. There are two reasons why not. (1) In the first place, there is the question what <u>constitutes</u> a "healthy" economy--roughly, the question of economic ends as distinct from means. And economists generally, I believe, would agree that that is not a question of technical expertise, but something more like a philosophical question: just our province, in fact. (2) And besides, there is, as has become increasingly apparent in recent years, considerable question both where ends leave off and means begin, and of whether the relation of ends and means in the area of national economies (again, by contrast with individual ones) is really an empirical one after all. Since I cannot devote space to arguing this point--which some may take to be obvious anyway--I will leave it to be, I hope, somewhat illustrated in the body of this essay.

In what, then, consists the "health" of an economy? In Western economies, at any rate, the standard view is that there are two main criteria: (1) full employment, and (2) price stability, that is, the absence of inflation. Other things could be said. For instance, it could be held (3) that maximization of the Gross National Product (GNP) is the supreme end of economic policy. And of course any number of national goals could be held to take precedence over any such economic considerations, to the point that economic policy becomes wholly subordinate to those. For example, a government might take certain religious goals to be overwhelmingly more important than mere material abundance, or anything like it. But we shall set aside all such possibilities here, for two reasons. First, we are assuming a secular society, and indeed assuming that governments have no business promoting religion, either in general or in any particular form. And a similar point could be made against any number of nonreligious ends that might be proposed for that role. Governments have no business building immense monuments either, in my view, even if they are momuments to the national glory. But second, apart from that we may take it that the purpose of this symposium is to inquire into economic ends specifically, leaving open the question whether it might sometimes be justifiable to subordinate those to some ends held to be more urgent, e.g., national defense. If we bear these two points in mind, then the ends of low unemployment and inflation, or of maximizing GNP, are eligible for consideration as "purely economic" in as reasonable a sense of that term as I can see at present.

I will also not consider the case of socialist economies, as such. It is, I believe, quite possible to interpret the criteria in question, including that of noninflation, for such cases, but to do so here would take us beyond what I take to be our purview. The economy we have mainly in mind is the American one, of course, but I shall take it that a suitable answer to our question would apply to any of the contemporary industrially advanced societies outside the socialist sector

—e.g., to the case of Canada, where this writer hails from.

The burden of the present essay will be to suggest that full employment, in a sense to be roughly established below, is really the supreme proper goal of national economic policy, by comparison with which neither the maximization of GNP nor price stability would count for much, insofar as they are really distinct things. They are, however, so closely connected that we would not often, I think, have to choose between them. However, let us consider them briefly insofar as they are distinct.

2. The Alternatives

(1) What about GNP? There is a tricky question here concerning the composition of the "national product." If it includes all and only those goods and services that someone wanted enough to buy them, then we can take this to be a reasonable measure of the national wealth, in one reasonable sense of that term. But so taken, a larger national product will, as I will argue below, be virtually indistinguishable from more nearly full employment. Taken in any other sense, however, there would be room to question whether the larger volume of goods and services really does represent a large volume of goods that are good for somebody, and services that do a real service to someone. In any case, if we take the idea of GNP abstractly, it seems perfectly possible that GNP_x could exceed GNP_y even though economy y had fuller employment than economy x. When that is so, I would insist, full employment is better, and will so argue below. But it would be surprising if it were really so unless the higher GNP was due to expenditures violating my stricture.

(2) Inflation is a more special case. If we take "inflation" to refer to a situation in which all prices, including interest (the cost of money, roughly), were rising at a uniform rate, it is obvious that the only disadvantage to inflation would be its inconvenience. But if full employment were maintained, that is all that it would amount to. It would certainly be inconvenient to have to bring a bushelbasket of money with one to the grocery in order to buy a loaf of bread, but that sort of problem can be cured by releasing new currency units every so often to reduce the volume of paper.

The phenomenon usually referred to as "inflation," of course, is not of that kind. What is normally so called is such that not all values rise at the same rate. Some persons will be on fixed income, and there will be long-term contracts made in good faith on the assumption that a dollar now is a dollar then. Such persons will suffer in an inflation, obviously, and in severe cases they could suffer mightily. But at some point, we might say that such people are underemployed; more precisely, we might say that their money is underemployed; it could do better elsewhere. Is this a semantic subterfuge designed to collapse two really distinct phenomena? Perhaps. But of course those who depend on incomes that depend on fixity of values are presumably doing what they want to do with their total resources, and a decline of such incomes below a certain point will force them to do something they did not want to do, viz., work. This is not what is usually called unemployment, but it is the underemployment of resources, personal resources. We shall continue this idea below.

(3) Full Employment. Why is this a good thing, and why is unemployment a bad thing? The latter is easy enough to say. Insofar as being unemployed is being without a source of income, it means that its subject will ere long face real hardship--lack of food, housing, and so forth. The person faced with a continually mounting number of zeroes at the end of every transaction done with money is not suffering a comparable decline. But this isn't the end of the story. In order to understand the special status of full employment as an economic goal, we need, however, to begin by trying to get a clearer view of what it is.

3. What is Full Employment?

One might suppose that full employment consisted of everyone's working "full time." But this is unsatisfactory for a variety of reasons. The first of these is that "full time" is a partly conventional concept. For some time now, we have thought of it as being constituted by the eight-hour day, or perhaps a bit less (9 to 5, minus lunch, say). But it was once much more, as we know, and it is easy enough to imagine its declining further: to six hours per day in a four-day week, for example. Obviously this concept of full-time cannot be spelled out simply by means of numbers of hours per unit of time worked.

And then there is the question what constitutes "work." It can hardly mean doing things for wages from a separate employer, since obviously self-employed people are employed (and many work many more hours per day or week or year than do employees of separate employers). It is, actually, rather difficult to pin down the idea of "work," but we shall settle for a rough idea. Let us say that one's work is what one does "for a living," as distinct from what one does for amusement or for self-enrichment and so on--though not meaning to imply that one is not to be thought of as working if one finds one's work amusing or self-enriching, etc. But activities engaged in solely for the latter reasons would not thereby count as "work." Work is a means, though not necessarily an intrinsically unpleasant one, and what it is a means to is, at a minimum, maintaining one's life. The vagueness of this, once one gets beyond utter essentials in the way of diet and the like, leads to considerations central to my argument, and will be adverted to further below.

But one major point remains. Consider a national economy in which three fourths of the population spend their mornings heaping large round stones into neat piles, and their afternoons disassembling those piles and returning the stones to their original locations. (A more up-to-date version: they spend their mornings working out elaborate executive or legislative prohibitions of various activities, and their afternoons processing applications filled out in triplicate for excepting the applicant from the morning's prohibitions--Sisyphus moved into the office.) Is this to be reckoned full employment, supposing that the government pays these people for these activities? I suggest not. What we surely want, under this heading, is full useful employment. At a minimum, useful employment is employment that produces something that somebody wants, over and above the paycheck which the worker, of course, wants. In the Sisyphusian case, no doubt the government wants "full employment," and so it is, in some sense, getting what it wants, and so one might say that somebody is getting something he or she wants. But it seems obvious that this does not count. Why not?

The reason, I think, has to do with the fact that governments are not "persons," and their wants are not, as such, the wants of persons. Given a popularly elected government, one presumes that when governments adopt and pursue various policies, those policies are designed to get someone or other something that that person wants or needs. But we must then distinguish between the desire of various people in the electorate <u>that</u> <u>there</u> <u>be</u> full employment, and the desire for the goods or services which would issue from the employment in question. The former desire, taken in and of itself, would seem very peculiar if it really was a desire satisfiable by the Sisyphusian labor we imagined above. Why not simply pay all those people their checks and be done with it, dispensing with the "work?"

We can imagine a peculiar case in which someone hires a person to pile and unpile stones in his backyard, just because of some weird aesthetic preference, or perhaps neurotic urge, of his own. This, I suggest, should count as "useful employment," even if bizarre. The public, <u>qua</u> public, does not inquire into the ultimate value to the soul of what consumers are willing to pay for. But we may be sure that most voters would not share such a peculiar preference. They would want people employed to some independently good purpose.

But most voters also, we may well suspect, would not be willing to pay for many of the alleged services of governments, if they had their choice about it as individuals and if the service were offered at the actual cost incurred by the government's providing it. This raises another issue, and an important one; but one we will not go into here. Instead, we shall make the charitable assumption that much government expenditure does get something that people want, and want enough to pay for at a rate at least within hailing distance of the costs involved in the form in which the State supplies them. But we may be sure also that there are appreciable numbers of cases where even that generous criterion would not be met. Employment engendered by such activities, I think, is not the sort we have in mind in supposing that full employment is a major goal of economic policy.

Next we must consider that some people would not want to work as much as others. Consider people who by preference take part-time jobs and reduce their expenditures accordingly:

they could work more, but they don't want to. In the extreme case, there are people who prefer to be hoboes, even in the absence of sufficient capital to afford them a modest living from investments. Should we say that these people are "employed?" It may seem unintuitive to say so; yet it seems clearly misleading to count them as unemployed. The unemployed should be those who would like to work but cannot, rather than those who simply do not like to work and have so strong a preference for that option that they are willing to exist at a very modest level in order to do so. Nor, of course, should we count those who prefer not working because they have sufficient capital to live off it at a level acceptable to them. But we perhaps should count those who, although in that condition, would prefer working if they could find a job that suited them; at least there is a question about them.

The question about these latter cases is brought sharply into focus when we consider the sizable numbers of people in North America currently living on unemployment and (sometimes) welfare checks. I do not have any hard statistics on the matter, and probably there are none, but it is clear that many in these categories are so, not because they can find no work at all, but instead because they can find no work of the type that they are trained to do, or that they feel themselves suitable for. Were these people not receiving these payments, they would likely broaden their concept of "suitable" labor: it is remarkable what we find ourselves able to do when starvation is the alternative. But Americans and Canadians do not think it dignified to do this. The sort of work that they might then find themselves doing is obviously only fit for persons of other races or nationalities. This is a rather peculiar sort of "unemployment"; and if, as is widely believed, the percentage of the unemployed who are in this category is very large, then the claim that these economies are not doing well, insofar as that claim is supported by unemployment statistics, must be taken with a grain of salt. But it is clear, at any rate, that such people are not employed in producing goods or services that other people want enough to pay for them at a rate acceptable to the supplier.

In the light of all these examples, how are we to define "full employment?" The trouble is that we can't say what one is tempted to: that full employment is the state of affairs in which everyone is usefully employed to the degree to which he or she would like to be. For we need to say something about background. We need to say, "...to which he or she would like to be, given his or her circumstances." The trouble is that the person doing nothing because there are no jobs available is employed to the degree he or she would like to be, given the circumstance that the only jobs available are ones he or she doesn't like enough to take, in those circumstances--circumstances that include the availability of unemployment compensation. To get around this difficulty, we must introduce a further condition: namely, that the subject is actually employed, in the sense that his or her income is derived from the sale of goods and services that person produces. This, too, is rough; but perhaps it will do for present purposes.

We now return to the question: Why is full employment an important goal of national economic policy? In order to answer this, we need to appreciate the significance of the idea of a national policy. Armed with an analysis of that idea, we will be in a position to complete the argument that full employment, understood as above, should be the sole aim of national economic policy, no other "priorities" being needed.

4. "National" Policy

Nations are different from people. A government has no separate interest. In particular, it is not an individual, although dictators sometimes act as if it were. Governments have no desires, needs, or views about the meaning of life. People have those, and the business of government must be, somehow, either to forward, or at least to maintain the conditions under which people severally may themselves forward, their life prospects in the light of their values. But just as governments have no goals of their own, so they have no income-earning powers of their own. Their money comes from you and me--from people. And so if governments attempt the former rather than the latter, that is, to promote people's good lives as distinct from merely making it possible for them to do so themselves, then there will be the possibility that it forwards the good lives of some at the expense of others who do not have the same vision, or who, even if they did, would prefer to be realizing it themselves rather than the others who would benefit from the more robust policy we are supposing. And this, on the face of it, would be wrong. A necessary condition for avoiding this, it seems, is that any policies promoting A at the expense of B must do so only at the temporary expense of B; B must, over the longer haul, benefit as well. And B must benefit more than he would if left to his own devices. (Those "own devices" include, of course, the willing assistance of whatever others B can enlist for the purposes at hand.) This is a tall order, and not easily met. Or at least, not unless we assume that governments provide an extremely valuable service--protection from the depredations of others, say--that nobody else can provide, and whose value is so great that the occasional policy working to the apparent detriment of some people is merely a modest price to pay for the overwhelming service in question. Since this is hardly the place to discuss the latter argument at length, I shall simply say that it is an assumption in this essay that the argument is trumped-up.

I shall also assume that people can, and often really do, come into rightful possession of various things, and of income. Thus I assume that when you coercively deprive someone of income or possessions, then you have, usually, done something wrong, and certainly always something that required special justification. Again, this is to gloss over enormous issues of detail, but I do not think that any contrary assumption makes much sense.

The net effect of these two assumptions is that governments need to show that their activities differ significantly from armed robbery of taxpayers, and that it is not very easy for them to do so. They should not, for example, attempt to play Robin Hood--indeed, it might be recalled that the object of Robin Hood's activities was itself a corrupt government, and his primary motivation the return of unjustly derived taxes to the people from whom they were taken. Modern Robin Hood theories, on the other hand, aim their arrows at private businesses that happen to have done reasonably well, with a view to redistributing the proceeds to the poor, even in the absence of any discernible claim to those proceeds. This is a form of favoritism, not justice. Or again, governments mount many of their programs in the name of insurance. But why, one must wonder, shouldn't people who want insurance be allowed to buy their own, or not buy any, if they prefer?

Thus if we look, in particular, at such economic measures as minimum wage laws and unemployment payments, or at the granting of rather extraordinary rights to labor unions, we should be wondering about the justifications given. When governments pay people for doing nothing, the effect is to make it impossible for employers to hire them at wages that make for a less attractive package overall than the unemployment checks constitute; and similarly for the minimum wage. Of if labor unions are assured by governments of the kind of clout that enables them to drive up prices artificially, then that amounts to a tax on consumers. It also amounts to a deprivation of economic liberty for those who would have been willing to work for the firms in question at lower wages than the union will allow. Indeed, until recently the officials of labor unions have tended to prefer the situation in which a smaller number of their own members are working, while the rest draw unemployment checks, to that in which large numbers are working, but at jobs other than, or wages lower than, they are accustomed to. In fact, it is by no means unheard of to have union officials preferring the situation in which nobody is working to one in which almost all of their members would be working, but at levels of wages deemed beneath the dignity of those officials to allow. But why should the rest of the public be forced to support the proletarian elite as against the rank and file of potential workers? Especially why should they when the result is higher prices and less people doing things that it would be worth some people's while to do? Can an economic policy having these effects be justified as a <u>national</u> one? Not obviously, it seems to me.

5. Full Employment

What's different about full employment? Let's start with the point of view of the typical individual: why would she or he regard it as desirable to be fully employed? Here we must realize that employment is not a good in the same way that a house, a car, a vacation, or any other consumable is. These things give us satisfaction, value. Of course a good job can do likewise. Just as a trip to the opera can be enjoyable and interesting, so too can be a job. But to evaluate a job in those respects is to evaluate it, simply, as a way of spending one's time. And independently of other factors, one's high evaluation of one's work can motivate one to spend nights and weekends at it. But insofar as it is a "job," what is distinctive about this activity is that it provides one with the means of obtaining the other things one wants, ordinarily by getting paid in money. For persons without independent means such as capital, to have a job is to make a living, as we say. And to make a living that consists in providing others with goods or services in a mutually agreeable exchange is to do this in a way that threatens and coerces no one, so long as the particular goods and services involved do not have harmful side effects. Circumstances, such as the fact that one's parents were not wealthy enough to leave one in possession of enough to provide a living independently of working, may "force" one to work; but no other individual forces you to. Nor does the "economic system" do so. The exchange system enables you to take advantages of such opportunities as there are, and indeed to create one's own, but it does not, nor is it required to, provide you with a living. That you must do yourself, with whatever help from you friends may be available.

But in such a system, why wouldn't an able person flourish? When he or she does not, having tried, it must be because no one else wants any of the services or goods that person would be able to provide. Yet when one considers how little in the way of sophisticated ability or skill it takes to perform useful services, this should be extremely surprising. Foreign immigrants to Canada with nothing but energy and reasonable health--lacking even the local language--soon are working as dishwashers, gas pump attendants, and the like, while their caucasian counterparts disdain such menial situations in favor of unemployment payments from the government. Why should the latter's complaints be accepted, in view of the former? A society in which A washes dishes for B, in exchange for a wage B is quite willing to pay, is surely preferable to one in which A performs no useful services to anyone while B pays taxes to enable him to do so. In the latter, not only is there less useful activity accomplished, and hence a lower real social product, but in addition some people are forced to use resources in ways they would prefer not to.

It will doubtless be objected by some that in the sort of society I am advocating, the incapacitated or constitutionally incapable will fare badly. But this is to raise a red herring. Our subject is the health of the economy, not of the sick. Sick economies are economies in which resources are underutilized, not economies in which nonresources are undercared for; and persons too ill to work are not resources. Others will make the more relevant complaint that in such a society, some workers are likely not to be paid as well as sympathetic and liberal academics would like to see them paid. For an academic, the minimum wage in any decent society will be somewhere around the Assistant Professor level. Or failing that, the very least that any employer can be required to do is to _marry_ their employees: to take them, that is, "for better or worse, for richer or poorer, until death them do part." That the employer in question may not be able to afford marriage--or even alimony payments, for that matter-- doesn't bother the intellectual. But it should bother the rest of us. For if the inevitable impossibilities from such a scheme are to be avoided, it must mean that as each industry so shackled slips beneath the surface, the government will be called in to keep it above water. Only it isn't real water, or perhaps we should say it won't really be above it! And as each profitable private enterprise is converted into an unprofitable public one, those very Assistant Professor proletarians will, as we know from others' experience, end up paying for it in the not very long run.

Full employment is the top national priority because _it is in everyone's interest_ to be as fully employed as possible, in the foregoing understanding of that expression. And it is in everyone's interest to _have_ everyone employed. Not only does this mean that one will not be saddled with the bill for their upkeep, but perhaps still more important, it means that there will be available to you the maximum array of goods and services that can be commanded with your resources _on a basis of mutual freedom_. The qualification might be important, for it is conceivable that you, whoever you are, would do better still if you could enslave at least some other people. It isn't likely, but it is conceivable. But I presume we may neglect that possibility. What matters, then, is that full employment means that the human resources of society are being put to the best use their owners judged it possible to put them to, the "owner" of a human resource being that human himself (or, herself).

Unemployment means that people who would like to be employed are not being so. It means that some people who would prefer to have the services they would provide at the price they would do it for are not having those services performed; and it means, in general, that other people are supporting them and, in doing so, using resources they would prefer, if they had their choice, to use in some other way. There is a widespread myth, originating with Marx, to the effect that it is in the interests of "capitalists" to have a large "reserve army of the unemployed" in society so as to keep down the wages of workers. This idea is remarkable nonsense, and it is the more remarkable that the myth continues to have currency among people who should know better. A "reserve army of the unemployed" is not in the interest of any "class" in a free-market society. Having such a body of persons on the loose means having a large body of persons with no purchasing power, and "capitalists," it should be recalled, make their living by selling things to people--notably, by selling goods that are mass produced. And it means that a sizable number of people, be it friends and relatives or public agencies, are diverting their expenditures toward the cost of necessities for those unemployed people, instead of using it to buy what entrepreneurs would want to sell them. It means, in short, that fewer capitalists are making less money than they otherwise might, as well as that many potential workers are doing less well than they would like to. In effect, unemployment will throw a burden onto capitalists, as well as others, who will have to be either directly or indirectly paying for the upkeep of the unemployed: directly through taxation if they are maintained by the public; indirectly through lost sales and slack business activity in any case. <u>Everyone</u> benefits from full employment.

Everyone benefits from full employment, and it is not clear that any other economic goal can make that statement. Protectionism, the artificial promotion of GNP, the maintenance of price stability at the expense of full employment (if that is a real choice, which I doubt), and the artificial redistribution of goods and services in the interests of one or another special class of people, such as the poor, are cases in point. The latter is the most popular among liberal academics. In their view, justice is taken to consist, for economic purposes, in "equality," or something close to it, this being the provision of equal incomes for all at roughly the Associate Professor level, regardless of prevailing supply or demand. I shall not here review the a priori case for this curious view,[2] which seems to consist mainly in a misinterpretation of the entirely correct idea that justice requires treating everyone in accordance with the same fundamental principles, hence "equality." But obviously the achievement of equality in the economic sphere, while not impossible in principle, is highly unlikely in a free market society; and so if you still insist on that goal, you will have to achieve it by force. And bringing that goal under the rubric of "justice" automatically sanctions the use of force when necessary, in my view;[3] so of course the force will be forthcoming. And thus when sizable firms or whole sectors of the economy prove to be inoperable at their current input costs (mainly wages), given the current state of demand for their products, the remedy to which advocates of this kind of "social justice" always turn is Government action: to shore up the wages of some by taking money from the pockets of others via taxation, or to finance retraining with tax-derived grants, in which case the decisions about what sort of retraining to engage in are made, of course, by highly-paid bureaucrats instead of by consumers. And so on. The end result is always the same: the enforced devoting of large amounts of human energy to the production of things that nobody really wants that much, or to the production of nothing at all; or, of course, to the production of things that are downright dangerous, such as ICBM's.

It would be easy enough to submit a list of "economic priorities" in the sense of things I would like to see lots of your money spent on. Among my favorites, for instance, are noise pollution, which is rampant in modern society, and visual pollution, as exemplified by rows of steel-framed electric towers marching across the countryside, and so on and so on. But the question is, why should my views count? Or anyone else's, in particular? (Or rather, how should they count? For each of us who feel that way can do a little bit about his or her favorite priority, when it comes to that.) But the point is that perhaps such questions should not be settled by political processes at all. I am not happy about having my list imposed by a minority, but I would also be unhappy about having it imposed by a majority. Why not instead let each person make his or her economic decisions in accordance with such wisdom and guidance as that person is willing to go by, letting the chips fall where they may? (Of course, we require them to clean up the chips if they fall in other people's yards!) This would admittedly have the almost intolerable consequence that a good many people would probably not end up doing what current social thinkers would like to have them doing; but then, that is almost inevitable anyway, and this idea does have the perhaps counterbalancing virtue that at least those people would be doing what *they* want to do, under the circumstances. Perhaps that should be enough.

University of Waterloo

NOTES

1. This paper was presented, in its original form, under the title "Do We Need Priorities?" at the session on "National Economic Priorities" at the Bowling Green State University Applied Philosophy Conference, May 4, 1984. I would like to thank several of those present for thoughtful criticisms, some of which have prompted modest changes in the present text. The ideas presented here are, however, essentially the same as in the original version.

2. But I do so at some length in a forthcoming paper, "Liberty Vs. Equality: Advantage, Liberty," to appear in *Social Philosophy & Policy*, Vol. II, #1, Autumn, 1984.

3. I have defended the connection between justice and force in various papers, notably in my "Pacifism: A Philosophical Analysis," *Ethics,* 1965 (perhaps more accessible in such anthologies as James Rachel's *Moral Problems* (3rd Edition: Harper and Row, 1979).

HOW CAN WE INDIVIDUATE MORAL PROBLEMS?

Onora O'Neill

To do applied ethics at all we need, it seems, not only adequate moral theories but something to which they can be applied. The likeliest candidates may seem to be moral problems which are unresolved, or inadequately resolved. On inspection this answer does not seem quite satisfactory. One way in which it can unravel is this: when we ask people what the most important moral problems are we will get varied lists. A little historical or anthropological reflection reminds us that what now seem major problems have not always struck thoughtful people that way. The concerns of feminists have been marginal in past ethical thinking, and in many societies abortion has seemed a trivial issue. Concern about animals has been a recurrent but not a constant theme in ethical writing. Concern about collaboration, resistance, keeping hands clean and civil disobedience has been prominent during wars, including cold and civil wars; but less so at other times.

An initial reaction to these reminders might just be the comment that moral problems do indeed vary, and so different problems are discussed at different times. But this is only part of the story. Slavery, serfdom and forced labor were not new problems, but newly perceived as moral problems. Behavior to distant kin may not seem to us a domain of acute moral problems, but others might see in this our moral blindness rather than lack of problems they took seriously. It seems that moral problems can exist unperceived and unheeded. A great deal of the effort of moral reform is to make others aware of and responsive to problems rather than solutions. The anti-slavery movement had first to show that there was something to discuss. It is always a move forward to get others to see matters in a different light and so "on the defensive."

The thought that moral problems can exist unperceived suggests, perhaps, a picture of incomplete discovery. Just as islands or rivers may exist uncharted, so perhaps there are undiscovered moral problems waiting to be entered on the map of applied ethics. But this analogy can mislead. Rival cartographers use different projections and conventions but do not disagree about the major topographical features of the region to be charted. But rival moral theories and outlooks may differ about what problems there are. The point is not merely that observation will pick out items only in terms of the categories brought to an inquiry. In that sense even the data of geography are theory led. Moral problems are theory led in a deeper way. The features physical geographers survey and map are agreed upon between them and are in many cases salient for non-specialist observers. The range of problems picked out by one moral theory may not be problems for adherents of different theories, and are not generally salient for non-specialist observers. It is hard to think of relatively specific situations that would be universally seen as moral problems; at most there may be universal agreement that problems arise in various broad areas of human life.

In the light of a moral theory concerned with rights, violations of privacy may seem serious problems; yet some may be invisible in the light of a theory concerned with costs and benefits rather than rights. In the light of one account or autonomy, relationships between "clients" and either prostitutes or social workers may seem standardly unproblematic unless we suspect failure of informed consent. In the light of other views it may seem that relationships with prostitutes or social workers, in their professional capacities, would always be morally problematic. It seems unlikely that there is any theoretically neutral way to establish a list of moral problems or even of the moral problems of a given period or society or of a specific domain of life. Rather any listing of moral problems will be theory led in at least two respects. Problems will appear on the list only in the light of theories which include appropriate concepts and will not be salient in abstraction from such theories.

There are those who claim that moral problems are theory led in a third and more fundamental way, in that they are not merely selected and made salient to us by theories, but exist only when the adoption or dominance of a certain moral theory or outlook establishes an agenda of moral problems for a given society. Such views may see moral discourse and the problems, arguments and solutions which such discourse permits and generates either as reflecting dominant ideologies or as a human invention. In these perspectives it would be senseless to claim that the same moral problem might be addressed by any of a variety of theories, or that certain moral traditions were blind to a particular sort of moral problem or that there is any objective list of "the moral problems" faced by any individual or society. All such claims make sense only if moral problems are to <u>some</u> extent independent of theories, even if our apprehension of them is theory dependent. They lack sense in a perspective which sees moral problems as constituted by a mode of discourse, and so not individuable in abstraction from that discourse. To those who hold such perspectives the current preoccupations of writers in applied ethics reflect no more than the internally generated difficulties of certain ethical positions which have come to dominate public discourse in certain societies. Liberal theorists debate the fine points of liberal ideology in a new scholasticism, and like earlier scholastics mistakenly see their debates as having a universal significance. But the problems they debate are only shadows of received theory and lack autonomous reality. While such perspectives localize others' moral debates, claiming that they lack sense beyond the context of locally received theories, they leave fundamental practical and moral questions formulated but not readily resolvable. For those who do not embrace a radical conceptual relativism it makes sense to ask whether one rather than another mode of moral discourse ought to be adopted, and to wonder whether certain theories are deficient because they fail to select or make salient problems of various sorts. For present purposes I shall set aside positions which embody a radical conceptual relativism and consider some of the implications of the claim that moral problems, even if not theory-constituted, are nevertheless only selected and salient in the light of some moral theories.

Even this limited sort of theory dependence has interesting implications for methods that can appropriately be used in moral reasoning. For example, it suggests that it is suspect (though it seems to me common) to start with some moral problem which is taken as "given" and then cast around for a fitting theory. A moral problem is not like an awkwardly shaped child, all too solidly there, while the parent casts around for a garment that will fit. When we find that utilitarianism sits awkwardly on a problem it is not enough to reach for a Rawlsian or a human rights outfit. For if we find that one of these is better suited, it may reflect only a match between the terms in which the problem was tailored and the terms of the theory. It might yet be that different articulations of the problem would fit it to be handled by other theories. Whereas a child has a given shape and clothes must be found which fit (more or less) well, a moral problem may be rearticulated to fall within the scope and terms of a theory to which it was initially ill-suited. But children cannot be reshaped to the clothes that are to hand.

But if moral problems are not "given" in a way which would make such patterns of reasoning possible, then a central problem of applied ethics must be to pick out the most important problems for applying moral reasoning. We cannot just wait for moral problems to "crop up" but must try to see whether those problems which strike us as important are indeed so, and whether current debates neglect other problems of moral significance. What reasons can we give ourselves for thinking that we are not overlooking central moral problems, as we now may think the generations who interpreted the rights of man as the rights of men or overlooked the iniquities of slavery did?

One reason that could suggest that we are no longer so myopic is that we now have a flourishing tradition of debate in applied ethics. If ethical theory is already being applied to moral problems, then we must already have methods for picking them out and for settling disputes about rival specifications of the moral problems of a domain. Only given such methods, as well as adequate ethical theories, could the enterprise of applying ethics take place. With this hope in mind I shall consider whether recent writing in ethics provides us with models for individuating moral problems.

Hypothetical Examples in Contemporary Ethical Writing

The surface of contemporary ethical writing is studded with detailed accounts of moral problems. Few writers now illustrate their theoretical claims with minimal accounts of the relations and transactions between A, B and C. Even Smith, Brown and Robinson, who used to serve so frequently, have been retired, sometimes with complaints about gender and class bias. Elaborate and detailed examples are employed in their place. I shall consider a sample of contemporary uses of examples in ethical writing to discover whether any offers or suggests a model (or an account) of how we might individuate moral problems. This section will be concerned with hypothetical examples, and the next with actual cases.

Sartre is often acknowledged as a pioneer here. His famous example of the young man torn between joining the Free French and staying to care for his mother ostensibly shows that moral codes and theories can neither make our decisions for us nor guide those decisions. The example is rich and detailed; but for all that, it is not independent of moral theory. Rather, it is constructed to make vivid the claims both of personal devotion and of wider public duty. The point of the example would be lost on anybody who did not appreciate both codes. The example is indeed not merely illustrative, but rather specifically illustrative of two codes which in this situation generate incompatible prescriptions. Here illustration is used to criticise the codes and more abstract theories it illustrates. Certain moral theories are shown to generate problems which they cannot solve. Sartre's aim is to cast general doubt on the adequacy of moral theory; yet his thought depends on the theory which provides the method of discerning and making salient the predicament discussed. The example shows at most that moral theories are incomplete and not that they can be jettisoned. For those who reject or do not understand the two codes to which Sartre's protagonist is drawn there is no moral problem here. Rich and poignant examples too are theory led. If Sartre's discussion leads us to doubt certain theories, it may also lead us to doubt the principles of individuation by which his crucial example was generated.

Rich and detailed examples have also been demanded and discussed in much Wittgensteinian ethical writing. Winch has even suggested that examples rather than theories are fundamental for moral thought:

> All we can do, I am arguing, is to look at particular examples and see what we do want to say about them.[1]

Curiously, the "particular examples" of much Wittgensteinian ethical writing are not usually examples of actual cases at all, but rather hypothetical, usually literary, examples of moral vicissitudes. There is, perforce, little we can do about such examples except "see what we do want to say about them." We cannot be guided just by looking at literary or other hypothetical examples for two reasons. First, if we have reason to think that moral problems are not salient in abstraction from theory, the results of looking will vary with the ethical theory or code or outlook through which we look. Secondly, focus on examples cannot guide our judgment of the fit between actual cases and supposedly relevant examples.

The first of these points is accepted by some Wittgensteinian writers.[2] They take it that whatever moral theory is embedded in current social and moral practices provides categories which select and define moral problems and considerations and render them salient. But if current practices determine the selection of moral problems, there is much less to insistence on detailed examples than the passage above suggests. Examples are not replacing theory in moral reasoning. Rather theory is present from the start, embedded in current practice. But if we think it possible to criticise current practice, we will not be likely to take it as defining what moral problems there are. Only a strong relativism which holds that current practice constitutes the domain of moral concern (rather than rendering one or another aspect of that domain salient) can take for granted whatever specification of moral problems current practices offer. Yet Wittgensteinian writing, even when it repudiates relativism, has said little about ways in which disputes about what moral problems there are might be resolved. Clearly no mere appeal to examples can avoid relying on some theoretical claims to justify a particular construal of the domain of moral problems.

Detailed examples have also been much discussed in post-Rawlsian writing in applied ethics. Appropriately in this genre of ethical writing we find discussion not only of hypothetical and literary examples, which are evidently theory led, but of actual case histories. The implications of introducing actual cases will be discussed in the next section. The special role of hypothetical examples in the Rawlsian method of reflective equilibrium once again offers us no method for individuating moral problems. Reflective equilibrating requires us to weigh a (tentative) ethical theory with "our considered moral judgments." In the process both theory and considered moral judgments may need revision. But considered moral judgments are themselves theoretical. They do not reflect direct access to an objective construal of the domain of problems. Rather reflective equilibrating is a method by which we can achieve coherence between our more specific and more general principles. Even when coherence has been achieved we may still worry whether the resulting theory fails to select certain types of moral problems, or gives undue prominence to others. Only if we thought that our initial, pre-reflective moral judgments embodied some direct intuition of moral reality could we be sure that the theoretical position reached with their help was neither blind to some moral problems nor hypersensitive to others. Reflective equilibrating is a method for constructing moral theories and not a guarantee that the most important moral problems have been picked out.

A focus on hypothetical examples is not a theory of moral individuation or of moral judgment; still less is it a way of breaking free from moral principles, codes or theories. Examples may be used to illustrate or to question moral theories, or to present them in less abstract and more socially contextualized ways. But no amount of vivid illustration or sensitivity to the contexts of moral reasoning can substitute for an account of why certain (but not other) situations are thought of as moral problems. The change in flavor of much modern ethical writings has been more like the shift from cookery books with black and white illustrations to cookery books with glossy colored photographs of meals that might be made. But the aim of applied ethics is not to illustrate recipes. It is more like helping a cook who has to decide what meals to produce when faced with actual utensils and ingredients, so needs to begin with an inventory of a particular kitchen and larder. Vivid illustrations are no guarantee of substantial results--especially when the utensils and ingredients illustrated are lacking.

Actual Cases and Ideology

Each of the moves towards more determinate and vivid ethical writing considered in the last section uses <u>hypothetical</u>, unavoidably theory led, examples for theoretical purposes. These moves neither show how we can justify a particular way of specifying a domain of moral problems, nor how theory is to be applied to the resolution of actual cases. So it may seem that if we are to consider how applied ethics is to be done we should look at actual rather than hypothetical examples and perhaps try to contribute to the resolution of actual moral problems. A good part of post-Rawlsian activity in applied ethics especially in the United States has been involved with actual, especially public, problems. William Ruddick has described some of these activities:

> In the last decade many academic philosophers in the United States have "gone public". In television interviews, newspapers and neighbourhood meetings they have discussed misuse of animals, whistle-blowing and world hunger. Philosophers sit on presidential commissions on medical experimentation, on scientific research review boards, on committees to draft codes of conduct for trial lawyers, social workers and senators. They consult with town planners, prison officials and inmates, generals, corporation executives, and hospital staffs. They run for political office, serve as congressional legislative aides, cruise in police cars....[3]

Philosophers who join in these activities appear to have no difficulty individuating moral problems; they have begun to work for morally adequate resolutions. But we may still wonder whether applied Rechtsphilosophie will be helped by cruising in police cars, or more generally by "going public." One result of such involvement is that the preoccupations of various practitioners may be taken to define the domain of moral problems. Applied ethics then runs the danger of allowing its agenda to be defined by the concerns of various interest groups and bodies of professional opinion. An agenda constructed on these principles may make some problems more salient than they would otherwise have been and may leave others invisible. Ruddick points to the danger of the "legalization of philosophy," which is revealed not only by the extent to which "public issues are defined by current court concerns," but also by a preoccupation with rights and violations of rights and relative lack of concern for matters such as the virtues of public life. The worldly success of applied ethics in the United States has to some extent been achieved at the cost of the restriction of focus which working with practitioners requires. It has also produced in some other parts of the English speaking philosophical community an uneasy sense that a great deal of the literature in applied ethics is either openly or subliminally structured by legal and social categories that are at home mainly in the political and ideological setting of public life in the United States.

A case can be made for accepting this restriction of focus. Many moral decisions, above all those of public life, must address problems as conventionally defined. They cannot await social transformations or revolutions which would reconstrue these problems. Rechtsphilosophie is unavoidably concerned with problems that arise under morally imperfect conditions, so must accept that the solutions it seeks are restricted in certain ways.

But there is also a good case for not accepting this restriction and so for not becoming too involved with practitioners. Conventional ways of specifying the problems of a domain are bound to miss problems which reflect the conventions themselves. For example, bureaucratic structures and the corresponding official discourse will not pick up problems which arise from the moral distancing of officials from cases with which they deal. Such distancing is basic to bureaucratic culture--the guarantee of impartiality--and its moral cost will therefore be little stressed within bureaucratic discourse. Yet this very distancing transforms other human beings into "cases" or "clients," which is surely not morally insignificant. Sometimes sharing practitioners' perspectives may be question begging or even corrupting. This may be the cost of allowing the agenda of public moral problems to be determined by the discourse and interests of practitioners.

One response to these difficulties might be to seek involvement not only with "establishment" practitioners in a given domain, but also (perhaps primarily) with those who dispute professional or official construals of some domain of problems. For example, some feminists have objected to the construal of childbirth as a standard medical episode in which patients are dealt with by professionals. They insist that women giving birth are not passive, hence not patients, and that they need medical help in the way that those attempting hazardous sporting or endurance records need medical help-- that is on stand-by. This external critique has affected some medical practices; for example, women in labor may be seen less as patients and less often obliged to adopt the prone and painful position needed by patients on operating tables, and may be allowed more choice and more information about their treatment and less social isolation than used to be thought necessary.

Involvement with practitioners does not have to be only with established and official practitioners and their perspectives. But it is unclear whether involvement with any or with multiple groups of practitioners can guarantee adequate specifications of the problems of a domain. May not involvements with practitioners yield rival specifications of the problems of a domain where practitioners are ideologically divided? And when there is consensus among practitioners, may it not still reflect an ideological position which is incompatible with whichever moral theory is being advanced as the most adequate approach to the resolution of problems? And may this moral theory not then also come to be thought of as one more contender in the ideological arena, which affords no privileged vantage point on the specification of problems or on their resolution? Such a line of thought might lead to the view that political activity must always not only supplement but precede moral reasoning, since we cannot rationally arbitrate between alternative modes of moral discourse, nor between alternative accounts of what problems there are. Once one or another ideology is established as dominant, applied ethics will be possible, though confined to the framework established by this ideology. If liberal modes of thought remain dominant in some places we can expect an applied ethics concerned with violations of rights; if liberal ideologies lose their dominance, concern with rights and their violation may fade from the agenda of applied ethics to be replaced by concern for whatever problems are made salient by the newly dominant mode of discourse. If such an account is correct, applied ethics is neither impossible nor unimportant, but is always less fundamental than political activity. Only political activity can establish a context in which certain moral problems become salient and certain solutions defensible or rejectable. Further, moral reasons could not then be given for activity that aims to reinforce or to undermine the position of any such framework of thought. If discourse (or ideology or received practices) constitute moral frameworks, moral reasoning can say nothing for or against imposing or seeking to impose a particular mode of discourse.

This picture of applied ethics as ancillary to dominant ideologies would not be widely shared by those who write in the field. The reasons why philosophers have sought public involvements has not been (merely) so that they could join in political struggles or so that they could elaborate the ethical implications of dominant ideologies. The hope has rather been to resist any claim that moral theory is just one of multiple contending ideologies, and to offer a distinctively philosophical contribution to the resolution of moral problems. But it is not enough for writing in applied ethics to seek reasoned resolutions of problems, while assuming that the specification of problems is given. It is also necessary to offer reasons for accepting a specific account of the morally significant problems of a domain. In the next section of this paper I shall offer some comments on what the reasoned specification of moral problems might minimally require.

Strategies of Reflection

If the enterprise of applied ethics is to do more than clarify and resolve problems raised by whatever ideologies become dominant from time to time, we must have at least some ways of questioning and revising proposed lists of moral problems. This need may seem easily met if we assume as our own starting point a particularly strong moral theory. For example, utilitarianism includes principles for individuating acts (in terms of expected consequences) and for individuating acts of moral significance (in terms of the expected utility of consequences). Given this theory we might expect a few difficulties (of principle) in discerning the moral problems of some domain, or indeed in calculating morally required solutions. Utilitarians do not generally need to consider or debate others' views of what the morally significant problems are; ideological divergences are of import only if they affect expected utility; their discussion is morally required only when such a debate will have beneficial consequences. But this absence of difficulties of principle is matched by difficulties in the practice of applying utilitarian thinking in actual situations, and framed by a lack of reasons for those who do not find themselves at utilitarian starting points to think utilitarianism itself more than a sporadically dominant ideology.

For those who cannot accept or justify utilitarian starting points there is no ready chart of the problems to which moral thinking should be applied. The difficulty arises, I think, from two quarters. First, without consequentialist principles of act individuation we are immediately faced with multiple distinct ways in which the situations and available acts of any domain can be picked out. Second, even when we can agree which situations obtain and which acts have been or might be done, we may still disagree over which are morally significant. Applied ethics needs moral theories which not merely pick out acts and aspects of situations as morally significant, but offer grounds for thinking that what the theory picks out is indeed morally significant. Adequate moral theories must include a critical appraisal of their own strengths. Without such theories we risk merely accepting or positing what moral problems there are, and do nothing to overcome the suspicion that applied ethics is only the under laborer or handmaiden of some possible ideology. To overcome this suspicion we need some account of what it would be to specify a domain of moral problems in ways that could be defended beyond circles to whom these problems are immediately salient. I shall offer a tentative sketch of some standards for such a critical moral theory.

First, it seems to me, any principles for picking out moral problems which are relevant in practical reasoning must start from the ways in which the agents who are mainly involved would construe the problems. (This suggests that it might be important to ride in police cars: but also to listen to those who commit, suffer or fear crimes). Construals of problems which neglect agents' views risk being unintelligible to those who may have to act. Our "moral starting point," to use a phrase of MacIntyre's, must include construals of acts, situations and problems which are intelligible to agents whose construal of problems may seem deficient or ideologically biased.

Second, it seems to me, rationally defensible principles for picking out moral problems need not pick out just those problems which those most affected or those best placed to act would initially and unreflectively pick out. A mafioso might view his main problems as those of enforcement and loyalty within the "family." Few would share his view. If applied ethics is not to be subservient to local or dominant ideologies it must sometimes reject both agents' and more generally received construals of problems as deluded or inadequate. But such rejections will carry weight only when alternative construals of problems are in principle rationally defensible to agents who may initially have been gripped by some ideology which rendered the proposed revised account of a domain of problems invisible or irrelevant. If we cannot sketch what such a defense of a way of construing the moral problems of a domain would be, and how it might be presented to those who face these problems, then we must, I think, concede that applied ethics can be conducted only within whatever ideological framework is taken to set problems and to define what would count as solutions. However, we may not always convince those who initially reject a revised construal of a domain of problems.

The task of defending one rather than another construal of moral problems need not, however, be that of establishing one rather than another fundamental categorical framework. It requires that an ethical theory, its fundamental moral categories, and the resulting specification of a domain of moral problems be defended in terms accessible to those who do not initially hold this theory. But such a defense may need no bridge between incommensurable conceptual frameworks. The task is rather to show that a group of human actions, relationships and possibilities, should be seen as constituting one rather than another sort of moral problem. It therefore seems that applied ethics needs something like what Kant called "reflective judging," where "the particular is given and the universal has to be found for it."[4] The first step in applying any moral theory is to reappraise or reconstrue not some indeterminate, conceptually alien, subject matter, but rather human situations which are already seen in certain light. It is because human situations are already, pre-reflectively, described in specific (no doubt partly ideologically determined) ways, because we have moral starting points, that it is possible to aim for a reasoned defense of one rather than another construal of moral problems, and for a reasoned revision of initial views.

Such a reasoned account of the moral problems of some domain must do more than offer a prepackaged (official or countercultural) construal of problems. The dominance or obscurity of the conceptual framework in which a problem is construed can be relevant to the ease with which a particular construal of some domain of problems can be communicated; but dominance neither confers nor precludes authority. Standards for reflective judging cannot be read off received outlooks or accepted practices or individual convictions and attitudes.

Rather reflective judging "stands in need of a principle." According to Kant when we judge a given particular reflectively we aim to discern the "coherence of experience with our own and others' cognitive capacities."[5] This provides some indication of ways in which construals of problems might be rationally defended even to those of differing outlook and ideology. To show a construal of some moral problem acceptable we have to show that it coheres not with the actual views but with the cognitive capacities of all who are party to the situation. The enterprise of revealing coherence demands an account which recognizes disagreements between rival ways of picking out moral problems and provides a background against which such discrepancies are themselves comprehensible. But this background does not have to include any Archimedean rational standpoint from which all possible disagreements can be resolved to the satisfaction of all possible parties. What is (minimally) needed is some shared strategies, to which all actual parties are committed in their own debates about the construal of problems within their own preferred ideological frameworks. Given this much we can make some moves forward. For example, if certain psychoanalytic construals of patients' behavior are to be preferred to patients' own accounts, it is because we can give some account in which both the subjective and the psychoanalytic account and the discrepancies between them are intelligible, and potentially intelligible to the patient. Or if we reject a construal of some family problem in terms of conflicting parental rights and children's claims, in favor of a construal which sets the matter in the context of a developmental account of the shared life of a family, this could be argued for only in the context of a larger picture within which the adversarial, conflicting rights model of family life is shown less coherent with what all parties can understand than the developmental approach. Ideological starting points are on this view essential to applied ethics, not because they constitute frameworks to which moral problems and their solutions are confined, but because a rationally defensible account of the moral problems to be faced must acknowledge and judge between the alternative construals of problems and situations from which those who have to act begin their debates.

If we were faced with <u>radical</u> conceptual relativism there might be no ways in which the discourse of those with rival ideologies could mesh, and so no strategies of reflective judging by which to tackle points of disagreement. But in the arena of human action this is not our situation. Gellner has recently commented:

> The incommensurability thesis owes something of its plausibility to a tendency to take too seriously the self-absolutizing, critic-anathematizing faiths of late agrarian societies, which indeed are generally so construed as to be logically invulnerable from outside and perpetually self-confirming from inside. Despite these notorious traits...the adherents of these faiths have, in practice, known how to transcend their own much advertised blinkers. They are and were conceptually bilingual, and knew how to switch from commensurate to incommensurate idioms with ease and alacrity.[6]

Radical conceptual incommensurability is not mainly a practical problem. Even when we come closest to it, and suspect others' sanity or our own, strategies of listening to the other may reveal levels of interpretability and decipherable communication. We can reserve our practical worries about radically incommensurable views of human action and moral theory for the arrival of genuine aliens; and if they arrive, they may turn out to be kin to E.T.

In calling the various strategies of reflective judging on which we may find agreement and the possibility of communication with others of disparate ideology <u>rational</u> processes, I do not mean to suggest that they are mechanical or algorithmic or that they guarantee any form of completeness or closure in our moral thinking. Presumably the very fact that alternative descriptions of situations are indefinitely many and that we have no calculus of descriptions means that reflective judging cannot be reduced to a set of algorithms. Strategies of reflective judging are no more than ways of revising initial construals of moral starting points to achieve greater intelligibility to the parties involved. The test of adequacy in such revisions is coherence with the cognitive capacities (not the actual cognitive performance) of those involved. If we follow such strategies we have no guarantee that we will start with any common agenda of moral problems, but some reasons to think that we may be able to move towards one, while acknowledging and making sense of discarded and rejected construals of the domain of problems we confront. If this is the case, then practical reason cannot neglect ideology, but need not be only its underlaborer or handmaiden. The specification of moral problems is no more in principle immune to rational criticism than is the formulation of moral theories.[7]

University of Essex

NOTES

1. Peter Winch, "Moral Integrity" in his *Ethics and Action,* (London: Routledge and Kegan Paul), p. 182.

2. Wittgensteinian writers who make this move include D.Z. Phillips and H.O. Mounce in *Moral Practices,* (London: Routledge and Kegan Paul, 1970); R. Beardsmore in *Moral Reasoning,* (London: Routledge and Kegan Paul, 1969); Rodger Beehler, *Moral Life,* (Oxford: Blackwell, 1978). I have discussed their approach more fully in "The Power of Example," *Philosophy,* forthcoming.

3. William Ruddick, "Philosophy and Public Affairs," *Social Research,* 47, (1980), pp. 734-48, esp. 734 and 744.

4. Immanuel Kant, *Critique of Judgment,* tr. James Meredith, (Oxford: Oxford University Press, 1978), p. 179. For further discussion of strategies of reflection see the last section of "The Power of Example."

5. Immanuel Kant, *First Introduction to the Critique of Judgment,* tr. J. Haden, (Indianapolis: Bobbs Merrill, 1965), p. 220.

6. Ernest Gellner, *Nations and Nationalism,* (Oxford: Blackwell, 1983), p. 120.

7. Earlier versions of the paper benefitted greatly from comments by R.M. Hare, William Ruddick, Richard Lindley, Keith Graham and Jan Narveson. I am grateful to each of them and well aware that the present version does not answer all the questions raised.

THE SAVINGS APPROACH TO SOCIAL CONFLICT

Bill Puka

What can philosophy contribute to resolving conflicts among the competing interests and ends of a pluralistic society? Which values have greatest legitimacy as public policy concerns and what priority should each be accorded relative to each other? These are the questions posed at this conference and in many other areas of ethics and public policy. It would be "just like philosophy," I think, to begin by questioning the apparent presuppositions of such questions. Should philosophy help resolve conflict over values or, perhaps, promote it? Should philosophy deal with values directly when it applies ethics to public policy, and should it order basic values like health, education, defense, and aid to the poor?

In the first part of this paper I will offer the view that philosophy should evaluate resolving, prolonging, and enriching social conflict over values together, without prejudgment. I will also argue that philosophy should deal with conflict over values indirectly, for the most part, by trying to handle deep conflicts between principles of right and justice and the divergent political ideologies they underlie. In Part II, I will present a method both for resolving such conflict and for stimulating constructive value conflict in both the ethical and political domain. Specific examples will be presented of how this method was used successfully to formulate an urban policy proposal and embody it in federal legislation. This legislation was introduced in Congress last year by Senator Gary Hart.

I

The drawbacks of intractable conflict in society, especially over aid to the poor, national security, control or de-control of the market, seem obvious to us. We must be reminded sometimes, however, that social conflict of this sort results from individuals expressing their liberty, pursuing their conceptions of meaning and happiness, and also striving to foster ideals of justice and benevolence. Active, non-violent conflict is a form of democratic participation in itself. Its process is likely to promote character development and responsible citizenship in a variety of ways, or so research indicates.[1] (The key is to structure conflict correctly.) By confronting the divergent views of others we often are caused to question and justify our own. Where conflict is perennial and concerned with basic values, we are urged to assume the viewpoints of others, to some extent, and to consider ways of accommodating divergent interests. Value conflict of this sort is perhaps the least dangerous way for a society to educate each new generation in democracy, pro and con. Thus, to <u>resolve</u> social conflict, especially from the top down, sacrifices many great moral-democratic goods. By contrast, philosophy is in an ideal position to <u>enrich</u> social debate over values in various formal and informal ways.

Moreover, if the discipline of philosophy has anything to offer regarding conflict in its own domain, it is hardly a model for resolution, and this is not for lack of methodical self-reflection. Primarily, philosophy models virtues of constructive conflict, of milking conflict for all it is worth, really, to deepen insight and refine conceptual skill, to make better philosophers and to better philosophical community.

Ethics has represented itself in public policy, thus far, primarily by applying general principles of right and justice to concrete policy problems. Most likely this approach has fueled conflict by offering utilitarian and Kantian solutions side by side without a reliable way to balance or order them. Were philosophers more able to say what their audiences should do with such accounts, aside from thinking them over, this approach could aid moral education, considerably raising the level of social debate over values. Yet the primary aim of many writers is not to fuel debate, but to propose policy, to render Rawlsian justice in distributing medical resources or to determine corporate liability for environmental harm. There is something puzzling and seemingly unreflective about this approach which deserves mention.

Presumably it is appropriate to apply the enlightened logic of philosophical ethics to the basic design of social organization, to the structure of a federal constitution, because so-called "non-voting" matters are involved. Here we look to expert opinion on the right and good, even at the risk of aristocratic paternalism, for fear of building mere conventions and prejudices into the bedrock of law. However, once we settle on constitutional morality and, let us say, on representative democracy as its preferred mode of implementation, particular visions of right, like particular visions of the good life, are supposedly no one's special province. They become types of interests or claims to be given equal standing, through their adherents, before the law.

An ethics of public policy, as opposed to a moral-political philosophy of the state, should prescribe that policies comply with constitutional morality. In a representative democracy, moreover, such ethics should advise legislators to inform their moral conscience philosophically and to represent the most reflective and widespread ethical stands of constituents in policy proposals. When we philosophers function as moral experts, however, applying effete ethical principles to policy issues, we do not take ethical representation seriously. On the face of it, our ethical advice is most suited to a benevolent dictator (philosopher king) or ruling aristocracy which need not take the ethical opinions of the populous into account. There is some justification to our helping social leaders provide enlightened leadership, given that most of our leaders are elected (and partly for that purpose) and that their policy proposals compete in the legislature. However, there are other roles to consider--tailoring policy proposals to interests groups or oppressed minorities, advocating an ethics for labor unions or for the spectrum of social sectors and interests.

Importantly, our accounts cannot be seen as neutral among these groups, in theory or practice. We do not offer objective moral wisdom to which all can adhere or aspire and around which social agreement can be ordered. Our accounts are conceptually accessible to the intelligensia primarily, and are most compatible with ethical views they already hold.[2] Though interest groups can hire members of this class to push their cause politically, effective lobbying will occur in the language and logic of its audience, the political leadership, not in the logic of constituencies. Moreover, most members of society do not have lobbyists pushing their ethical viewpoint in the public sector.

In this way, our philosophical accounts are actually tailored to centralized and authoritarian conflict resolution by social leaders. They cannot hope to reflect the varied ethics of the citizenry. In a representative democracy, these so-called conventional ethics must be represented somewhat, especially to the degree that they are stable, reflective, and sincerely held. They need not be philosophically valid or sophisticated to warrant standing. This is because we assume tacit consent to government policy, at least to its ongoing logic, and because the ethics of policies we are required to obey must be self-legislatable. (Here conventional ethics merit representation in a way that popular views on economics or sociology may not.) We cannot claim to be respecting members of our society morally, or to be governing "by the people," if policies fail to embody at least some of the people's actual views on what is right and just. Certainly a government would be remiss in its duties to foster social stability and morale, to motivate widespread commitment to just policies, if it did not assure that all citizens could see themselves (their actual interests and views) in the laws they obey.

Despite these drawbacks in current philosophical practice, applying general principles of right and justice to policy issues, as we do, is superior to handling particular values in a policy context. After all, philosophy is concerned primarily with the validity and generalizability of value judgments, with their consentability in policy. Therefore it should focus on the network of reasoning which can explain, justify and prescribe value choices, not on their peculiar content. Ethical philosophy should be concerned with values as they figure into the overall logic of ethical judgment. Interests and values which are stable and reflective, most likely to be valid, should be derivable from general rationales.

Unfortunately, ethics has encountered enormous difficulty over the centuries in evolving general value principles or rendering derivations of value from justice rationales in reliably discriminating ways. This has lent powerful support to the view that the content of particular values and value priorities is largely relative to individual tastes and group conventions and hence is too arbitrary and fleeting for either ethics or government to sanctify. Rather, most maintain, values are to be handled indirectly and impartially as the range of permissible goals of activities sanctioned by moral rights and democratic procedures.

Of course, only certain goods or portions thereof will figure into policies that are enforceable and subsidizable by government. Moreover, criteria of enforceability will more closely conform to the logic of right than value. Different portions of good will be enforced most appropriately at different levels of government, some constitutionally, others by federal statute, executive order, state or city ordinance, and so forth. How values are treated at each of these levels will depend somewhat on formal and situational differences of each jurisdiction. Thus an ethical analysis of a value's holistic importance will not be of great use in policy making.

Furthermore, our most important social values such as health, defense, and aid to the poor normally constitute shared requirements of social life. They are normally targets of rights or justice and are protected most rigorously in that form. Conflicts among such values should be handled as conflicts among rights which have a different moral logic than concern for (non-necessary) social welfare.

Lastly, any account which distinguished our most legitimate and important values would have to be tempered by our democratic duty to represent the views and interests of the citizenry, whether enlightened or not. The range of interpretations on values here will seriously dilute any subtle differentiation of values which a philosophical analysis might provide.

Though the foregoing considerations do not eliminate the need for assessing competing social values, they do mitigate against assessing them directly, using value standards. On these bases I propose that value conflicts in society be dealt with philosophically by wrestling with conflicts among ethical theories as wholes, between principles of right especially. I suggest also that conventional principles be thrown into the pot and that decisions concerning whether to resolve or promote value conflict through policy be based on the comparative merits or each as seen from the perspective of various sectors of society.

II

For almost two years I worked as a legislative aid to U.S. Senator Gary Hart. In hundreds of meetings with Congressional and Executive Branch staff, with interest groups, lobbyists, and constituents, I cannot recall confronting conflicts of ends, interests, or values in themselves. Rather such conflicts came packaged within the more striking structure of moral and political ideologies. Most everyone seemed to agree that the poor were badly off and needed aid and that national defense had to be financed. Aside from factual disagreements over the state of national health, poverty, or defense, I did not encounter great divergence in the importance given to these values. "They are all necessities, after all." However, in discussing what we should do about these values--what people can claim by right, what a government can enforce or subsidize, powerful differences in judgment came to the fore. The citizenry thinks about the ethics of public policy as philosophers typically do, that is, with value conflicts subsumed under justice and rights rationales. (Extensive research cited above supports this belief.) I suggest, then, that the slant I offer on how ethics should deal with social conflict over value is socially and politically realistic, that it will allow philosophy practical influence.

The method I devised for this purpose, the Savings Approach, was used successfully to design an extensive urban revitalization bill. "The Community Assistance and Revitalization Act" was introduced in both Houses of Congress in February, 1983. In outlining this approach here I hope to provide further grounds and means for skirting value conflict when designing policy.

As a method, the Savings Approach is deceptively simple, most usefully characterized as a short and motley list of commonsense steps. It directs us first to seek out general rationales or principles and break them down into component parts. These are then separated into different conceptual domains--ethical, moral, political, legal (constitutional/statutory)--and evaluated as assets or deficits regarding the problem at hand. This evaluation is based not only on intrinsic merits of the components but on their relative compatibility with the preferences or beliefs of contending parties and their usefulness as negotiating points. (Itinerant insights or tenets are sought also, then evaluated and added to the collection of assets and deficits in each domain.)

To complete this evaluation and move from points to

viewpoints, assets and deficits are to be combined in complementary ways, shifting their relative positions. Thus, a former part of structure becomes content, a former goal becomes a justifying rationale. Often a great defect in one view (a maximization rule, for example) may be just what is needed to fill gaping holes in another (a view which ranks right too strongly over good). It is important, therefore, to "save" defects as well as assets. In this way, also, the maximum number of currently held beliefs or interests is represented in the final view.

The process of reconstruction here should also seek transcendence; it should add something new and progressive rather than merely remixing old parts. In the savings approach, then, "third alternatives" to rival positions should be sought or generated which encompass components of contending views but defy assimilation to any.

Lastly, the Savings Approach requires an extra-theoretical accounting or a consistently high rating across its domains. A "third alternative" from the moral perspective must also be politically feasible and economically frugal, in the spirit of current legislative logic. Once the best views are assembled, based on these criteria, one or more may be advocated, depending on a further evaluation of the roles a philosopher should play and the effects s/he should intend in the social process.

Obviously, the Savings Approach aims at a delicate balance between representation and validity, progress and consensus. It tries to reflect the widest variety of beliefs and interests among contending groups, even where they seem dubious, by retaining them piecemeal and combining them in mutually ameliorating ways. At the same time, it shifts categories of debate through conceptual analysis and theoretical restructuring so that distinct sets of interests are difficult to hold in contentious formation. These new distinctions, ideas, and ideals also serve to edify partisan interests and inform merely subjective opinions.

The Savings Approach directs us to break general principles (which fuel conflict) into component rationales and then recombine them with an eye to complementarity. Since generalization is crucial to any ethics of public policy, the target of this directive must be overgeneralization. Overgeneralization is seen here as a primary source of conflict among principles. Where overgeneralization occurs in ethics, its most offensive form will likely be reductionism. I count as reductionist an attempt by one theory to account for all the claims or prescriptions of another or to account for the very structure of that theory as a set of its own claims or implications.

A realistic account of theory-building would see most normative and meta-ethical generalizations as pre-philosophical judgments, like particular intuitions which arise spontaneously through interpersonal interaction and commonsense reflection. The considered judgments from which we build a moral theory represent a system of moral thought in tact, which philosophy fills out, refines, and slants in various ways for the sake of validity.

At base, then, a philosophic ethic may begin as little more than a rule of thumb ("do what is best for everyone in the situation"), and together with a few insights (sometimes giving up something you want now gets you a lot more in the end, effects count more than intentions). Largely because of the way these views are generated in practice, the core of an ethic will favor a particular slice of human concerns and experience, a narrow slant on moral wisdom. Thus one ethic may emphasize the quality of experience rather than of actions or traits, focus on what rules do for society rather than what goodness is in an individual. It may be struck by the discontinuity between duty and going beyond it rather than the continuum between better and worse, even between better or worse injustice.

When one surveys major traditions in ethics, especially in view of long-standing objections to them, it is striking how each handles a favored type of case that the other can not. (Respecting individual autonomy equally is a problem for utilitarianism, fostering social progress for justice.) This is so despite decades of debate and internal revision among and within rival theories. Such observations lend support to the view that the origin of their divergence is limited perspective and that conflict among them has come from one theory trying to stretch itself, without retooling, into another's domain. (This tendency is a natural consequence of philosophical debate.) Thus, for example, a perfectionist principle might try to explain the logic and importance of the right to liberty on the basis that it fosters most effectively the power to develop one's virtues autonomously. To call such marauding, "elegance" or "simplicity"--one principle explaining the diverse range of cases--is misleading. It implies that universal principles are simplified versions of (or substitutions for) more complicated ones that did the same job. Different theories may simulate the same prescriptions, for the most part--a utilitarian theory can justify a set of rights, a principle of justice--but the way they do it makes all the difference. Partly this is because intentions count morally. To act on different principles, to respect rights because rights holders deserve it or because it will help society, makes a difference. Striving for elegance or simplicity in this way fuels needless debate. The proponents of one view rightfully will not accept the synthesizing of their pet prescriptions by a rival view as adequate explanation. Providing equal opportunity may increase social stability by curbing the resentment of the unemployed, but it is required morally, some would argue, to offset the morally biasing effect of inherited advantages in society.

It should be noted that even the most plausible attempts at logical reduction and elegance in ethical theory generate serious problems. Rawls' principles of justice, even though they are two (actually four, represented as two),[3] simply cannot accommodate just desert adequately nor its different components--desert by effort, production, marketable production, socially beneficial production. This shortcoming has generated extensive controversies at the most abstract levels of theoretical debate--the entire Rawls/Nozick controversy being one. At the level of applied ethics, however, the potential for conflict is much more serious. Here we do not want macro-rationales deemphasized, as Rawls characterizes his treatment of desert. Particular policy problems emphasize microfacets of the ethical domain, after all. The more elegant the principle, the less guidance it provides for well-tailored applications. Hence we are forced by elegance itself to resort to intuitive judgments and interpretations when applying principles to cases. This is precisely what principles were designed to avoid, according to Rawls. Suppose we assumed that universal principles of utmost elegance are only to be used at the most general and basic levels of application to society, or for explanation at the most abstract level, and that more specific rules are needed for more specific prescriptions. How could we reliably derive or relate such rules to these more general and pure principles if the rationale we require is, at best, only hinted at there?

An obvious way around such problems of reductionism and the conflicts they generate, is to break down general theories and principles into component parts and use them in their limited domains alone. Following the Savings Approach we also should try to combine these components in motley and complementary ways, forming theoretical hybrids in which the strengths of some components overcome weaknesses in others.

Obviously there are many ways to proceed. I began by consulting social research data on values, ethical choice and moral reasoning in American society. Again, this serves the representative, democratic functions of policy ethics. While American values showed great variability and relativity by socio-economic class,[4] the reasoning behind such judgments (where it was researched) showed much greater stability and commonality. There were clear rationales of egoism, just desert, social utility, individual rights, and (some) egalitarianism, with smatterings of duties to self and to self-development here and there.[5] A definite trend away from ethical egoism and toward more sociocentric perspectives seemed evident as well, with increasing age and education. On this basis, it seemed possible to represent public ethics in enlightened policy by using the range of philosophical traditions which popular ethics approximated.

Thus I formulated what Rawls called a "mixed conception." Optimistically I dubbed it the "Right Mix," building it out of the central principles of right from among the major ethical theories--individual rights, equal opportunity, just desert, social utility, and perfectionism. (One way around conflict is to accommodate a full field of competitors.) Again, these principles are the effete correlates to popular American ethics. Since each of these principles may handle only certain sets of cases and concerns well, as the foregoing theory of theory-building contends, they all must be circumscribed in scope, tailored to their proper domains. Only when pared down in this way will these priniples be more complementary than at odds. In addition, conflicts between these principles, which will arise no matter how we circumscribe them, must be handled by ordering them in theory.

By distinguishing the moral, ethical, political, and legal domains of these principles, as the Saving Approach directs, I found grounds for limiting the scope of each, and for ranking teleological principles, generally, below deontological ones. My analysis concluded that teleological principles are not moral principles per se, but principles of general value and prudence. They must be drastically and selectively limited in scope to match the more distinctive moral focus of deontology. The dominant trend of philosophical and popular opinion as well as the very ethical structure of the Constitution (rights over general good) seem to favor deontology over teleology. In a nutshell, they all recognize that it is more tolerable for a government to forego progressive social opportunities in order to defend individual liberties than to infringe individual autonomy for the sake of social progress. Moreover, attempts to order liberty over welfare within a teleological framework seem highly problematic.

Specifically, the Right Mix handles internal conflicts by ordering rights over equal opportunity, then just desert above moral perfectionism and, lastly, ideal-utility. Such a ranking guarantees an arena of autonomy for each individual to shape her or his life (even allowing egoism some sway) before questions of doing justice to others even arise. Once they do arise, however, one cannot take one's due, based on the relative merit of one's accomplishments, until the non-meritorious factors in one's accomplishments (the inherited portion of one's talents or social opportunities) are compensated for. Perfectionist duties are placed over utilitarian ones to help ease the burden of maximizing goods through the general storing of benevolent proclivities, and so forth.

While teleologists may appreciate being represented in a mixed view, they may feel that they are under the thumb of deontology in the above version. One way to handle the dominance of deontology above, would be to restrict the scope of rights and desert, as we restricted the scope of teleological value. After all, it is counterintuitive from a moral value perspective to restrict someone's attempts at benevolent aid, for example, in order to respect another's right to amass expensive and rarely used toys. (Here I assume that on most property rights theories I am duty-bound, morally, not to use your owned goods to aid the poor even if you have no use for them.) This traditional paradox of deontology seems irresolvable if we assume that all uses of liberty (including all productive acts) express the moral self, and that, therefore, rights must be maximally extensive within the bounds of equality. Both assumptions are unwarranted. The arena of autonomy that we must respects so unfailingly in each person should be defined selectively and narrowly, to capture only the equal essence in all of us. Additional tribute to our varied interests and pursuits can be exacted by less demanding, more morally conditional rationales. This lets telelogy in without deposing deontology.

It is crucial to notice that the Savings Approach does not guarrantee a satisfactory recvonstruction of ethical rationales. It only guides us in pursuing such a goal. Moreover, while any plausible "right mix" might be superior to any plausible reductionist, single-principled alternative, clearly a range of competing mixed conceptions can be generated and debated. The "right mix" logic sketched so briefly here is merely one first attempt at bi-partisan policy ethics. I present it only to hint at how a Savings Approach is practiced in the context of ethical theory.

A second such hint, this time of a "third alternative," will close our discussion. A "third alternative," as the Savings Approach envisions it, is a rationale that builds in the assets of rival principles and their combinations but transcends them in a way that reduces or enriches conflict. My example will be drawn from the policy and political ideology side this time, to help demonstrate the application of already Saved ethical principles, of the Right Mix sketched above.

Representative Jack Kemp and President Reagan sponsored a private sector enterprise zone approach to job creation and economic revitalization in urban ghettos. Basically it offers a variety of tax breaks to business owners (and investors) in exchange for the guaranteed employment of a certain percentage of poverty-stricken and unemployed residents.

For the most part this proposal for community assistance satisfies political conservatives and those who favor individual rights because it utilizes market mechanisms and relaxed market controls. It aids only the most needy, involving tax burdens that would be eased by decreased unemployment payments, new taxpayers joining the rolls, and increased profits which would increase taxpayer earnings. Under such conditions, just desert based on production (and probably effort) would determine salary and promotion, to a large extent. (The influence of natural talents and social opportunities provided by SES would be minimal given the poor quality of education and lack of job experience or training in ghetto areas.) Conservatives might point out to liberals, also, that enterprise zones would increase drastically the job opportunities of those who need them most and likely would increase job training as well. (The best job training is a job?) Surely most prospective employees in urban ghettos would have a relatively equal chance of being hired under zone provisions. To a significant extent, the zone approach also accords with Rawls' Difference Principle of Justice. It applies (tax) incentives to those most likely to increase economic prosperity in a way that benefits (here a job is guaranteed) those in greatest need. Providing jobs versus handouts also helps break the welfare cycle which undermines the equalizing effects of income for the poor.

Liberals take a dim view of enterprise zones, believing their incentives will most likely increase profits for already thriving businesses while providing a small number of mimimum wage jobs for residents. Their long-term effect, if successful, would be to price residents out of their own neighborhoods. Thus, tax subsidies would make the affluent better off at the long-range expense of the poor. Morally, liberals do not see a hope of more equal opportunity or economic power here.[6]

A "third alternative" in this context should seek to build on the assets of free market and moral aspects of the zone approach as a way of catering to liberal-egalitarian concerns as well. It should also go beyond the perspectives of these competing ideologies and underlying principles. Such a "third alternative" is found in employee ownership--Employee Stock Option Plans (ESOPs) and producer co-ops. It can be augmented, also, by a community owned development corporation or zone-GSOC (a second "third alternative" I generated from current provisions in the U.S. Tax Code). Together these provisions also help foster the teleological principles of "The Right Mix," focusing on moral perfectionism.

In CARA (the bill I authored for Senator Hart), tax incentives from the Kemp zone bill were retained, for the most part, but adjusted in various ways to favor businesses which were partially or wholly owned by their employees. Current tax advantages for selling percentages of stock to one's employees were increased also. In addition, a tier of cheap credit was made available in the zone (cheap for both businesses and taxpayers) by freeing up a small percentage of reserves at Federal Reserve Member Banks. Half of available loan funds would be earmarked for employee owned businesses. (Cheap credit is crucial but often difficult to come by for small or employee owned businesses.[7])

Employee ownership appeals to liberals because it decentralizes economic power and thereby fosters equal economic opportunity. Ownership rather than jobs also increases the likelihood of a more egalitarian power or management structure within the company, which extends into compensation and hiring policy. Leftists support employee ownership, especially in the form of producer co-ops, because it gives employees (equal) control or significant influence over their working conditions, schedules, and activities as well as their salary. It even helps them determine the investment and location policy of their company, and policy on social responsibility as well. In the zone, such ownership structure would decrease the likelihood of commercial abandonment and job loss through relocation or business failure which normally follows decreased profit margin in traditional firms. (Employee-owners will oppose relocation and will take pay cuts to keep their company afloat.) The higher productivity of most employee-owned firms also averts these evils. (Employers work harder for themselves.)

Conservatives also support employee ownership because it is a free market, non-distributive strategy to urban revitalization. In fact, it lightens taxes and other restrictions on business. Thus, it upholds the property rights of taxpayers and entrepreneuers alike. Employee-owned businesses compete like all others and succeed or fail on their merits. As owners, workers are drawn over to the side of management as well, and are "won for capitalism."[8]

In these ways, the employee ownership alternative deals with conflicting claims by accommodating almost all of them, and to a relatively equal degree. It is neither liberal, conservative, nor both, as a further look at its moral benefits will now help show.

The discussion above indicated ways in which employee ownership provisions comply with the moral dictates of conservative zone policy while abating liberal fears of injustice. For the sake of brevity, then, I will assume that the rights principle of "The Right Mix" has been satisfied[9] and that the equal opportunity principle has been partially fulfilled (by job and ownership opportunities provided). This leaves some opportunity trade-off problems to be resolved--why should employee ownership opportunities restrict the availability of tax breaks and credit for entrepreneuers who seek ghetto locations but do not wish to share ownership? It also leaves ideal-utilitarian questions open--if tax subsidies favoring ownership over jobs are justified, then why not limit tax advantages to producer co-ops or democratically managed companies? Though I will concentrate on how employee ownership fulfills the perfectionist leanings of "The Right Mix," a few comments should be made to support the role of employee ownership in equalizing opportunity.

To the extent that equal opportunity is morally justified, it is necessary to overcome the biasing influences of social class, local educational environments and the like, on access to debt and equity capital and entrepreneuership. While each individual cannot own a business, each may be able to share in ownership, and where a huge range of the best economic opportunities is tied to entrepreneuership, and its prerequisite, an equal opportunity principle must address these areas. Being a salaried employee, as opposed to a part-owner, severely decreases one's ability to express and develop some of one's most morally central and valuable traits in work activity. It becomes inordinately burdensome also, in general, to fulfill on-the-job moral obligations such as eliminating unsafe working conditions, opposing the unfair treatment of co-workers, and exposing illegal or socially harmful policy or production by one's company. Thus, equal access to capital and entrepreneuership need not be justified by an economic power (as opposed to liberty) argument (alone) but by a necessary-for-moral-responsibility argument.

As for moral perfectionism, employee ownership makes it much more likely that unusually democratic (non-authoritarian) management structures and interactions will occur in the workplace. It greatly increases the chances that workers (and management) will express and grapple with each other's viewpoints regarding how things should be done, how basic problems should be solved. Such institutional settings, aside from being moral ideals in themselves, are especially conducive to developing and expressing moral competencies and virtues which are needed to comply with moral and legal obligations self-legislatively. In shared ownership work settings, basic common interests are at stake. This causes employees to work toward understanding and accommodating each other's views, to mutual benefit.[10] The development and expression of such competencies and virtues is, perhaps, among the highest class of goods (as judged by their strong relation to principles of right). Moreover, since their development is necessary to self-legislated moral agency and to assumptions of tacit consent in a just democracy, they are legitimate targets for public policy support. (In CARA, these values are modestly subsidized rather than directly enforced. Thus, they do not violate the ordering of rights and justice over perfection and ideal utility.)

Since work occupies much of a worker's life, and since formal moral education is rarely provided in schools (nor especially effective for moral development, as defined here) the rate and degree of a worker's moral development will be determined largely in the work setting. Therefore, obligations to foster moral development will have to apply here.

I believe that these perfectionist considerations, when added to rights and justice arguments, strongly favor employee (and community) ownership policy over mere job creation.[11] Hopefully they also demonstrate some of the moral virtues of constructive conflict and amplify the bi-partisanship of a Savings Approach ethic and ideology.

Rensselaer Polytechnic Institute

NOTES

1. There is extensive research showing that conflicts over values are superior stimulants to cognitive role-taking and the sophistication of moral reasoning than formal instruction or reading in moral thought. See, for example, Blatt, M., "The Effects of Classroom Discussion on the Development of Moral Judgment," *Journal of Moral Education, 4* (1975); 129-161.

2. According to a wide range of psychological researchers, there is a strong correlation between degree of education, SES, and sophistication of moral reasoning. The moral viewpoints of more highly educated and affluent individuals, such as political leaders, more closely approximates theories of philosophical ethics than do ethical viewpoints of the less educated working class. Rather powerful evidence has been amassed to show that most of American society either does not comprehend the moral rationales of the American Constitution consistently, or assimilates them to rationales with which they are incompatible. See, for example, Rest, J., "The Hierarchical Nature of Moral Judgment," *Journal of Personality, 41,* (1973); 86-109.

3. Rawls' principles foster equal liberty, equal opportunity, equal welfare, and unequal use of incentives to foster general welfare.

4. See, for example, Rokeach, M., *The Nature of Human Values,* New York, 1971.

5. Colby, A., Kohlberg, L., Gibbs, J., Lieberman, M., "A Longitudinal Study of Moral Judgment," *Monographs of the Society for Child Development, 48,* #1 & 2, 1983.

6. Zone tax breaks will be most useful to large, well-heeled, capital intensive companies with large tax liabilities. Such businesses typically provide small numbers of new jobs and are likely to offer minimal salary and job-training. Some may be "bad neighbor" businesses which bring pollution and other dangers to a residential area. Once profits are taken, such businesses are likely to move on, abandoning their commerical properties and eliminating jobs. Small businesses cannot easily utilize zone incentives though most new jobs are usually created in this business sector. Should the lure of incentives attract such businesses to zones their already high failure rate will probably increase further. This will eliminate the jobs they create in the zone and add first-time recipients to the unemployment benefits rolls. Success for zone economies will spell displacement for ghetto residents since retail and rental prices will rise. Past experience with urban revitalization supports the view that its supposed beneficiaries are often made worse off in the long run. This undermines the supposedly bi-partisan virtue of a free market zone approach which is efficiency in generating benefits for all.

7. Those who favor co-ops have noted correctly that ESOPs often accord only token ownership and substitute stock for pension benefits. Stock in a single company is likely to be less secure than pension funds. Therefore employees may be disadvantaged by an ESOP maneuver overall. To help overcome these problems (which are often deceptions by management) I geared the bulk of zone tax subsidies to companies with at least 51% of voting stock owned by non-office holding employees. Note that a majority of ownership does not imply a majority vote (nor worker management) since workers may not vote in a block.

8. When employee ownership is accomplished under an ESOP, it requires very little tax assistance. It provides traditional owners with a new source of credit and a market for their stock. (Employees apply for credit jointly and transfer it to the company in return for stock.) Employees get the stock free. ESOPs also allow for degrees of partial ownership or gradual takeover by employees which make them more alluring to traditional owners and to Congress (where ESOP legislation has "breezed through" over the years).

9. Presumably, then, rights must be defined in "The Right Mix" so that they will not permit non-fulfillment of aid to the poor. Conservatives typically recognize such minimal obligations. It may be assumed that much aid to the poor in urban ghettos is owed as compensation for past injustice and for the sake of protecting political equality which is made vulnerable by severe economic deprivation.

10. Higgins, A., Power, C., Kohlberg, L., "Student Judgments of Responsibility and the Moral Atmosphere of High Schools," in W. Kurtines and J. Gewirth (eds.) *Morality and Moral Behavior,* (New York) Wiley Interface, 1983.

11. The community-owned development corporation I provided in CARA functions much like an ESOP and has the same moral explanation as employee ownership, in general. It would allow zone residents to compete with other real estate interests to "save their homes" or get in on condominium conversion. One compensation for being displaced is to collect high rent on one's former abode. The Zone-GSOC would permit that, in effect. It would also stimulate residents to cooperate and conflict constructively, regarding common concerns.

HONEY DRIBBLES DOWN YOUR FUR:
REMARKS ON ENVIRONMENTAL ETHICS

Tom Regan

> For Dogen, the others who are "none other than myself" include mountains, rivers, and the great earth. When one thinks like a mountain, one thinks also like the black bear, and this is a step...to deep ecology, which requires openness to the black bear, becoming truly intimate with the black bear, so that honey dribbles down your fur as you catch the bus to work.[1]

I imagine there would be more on my mind than the honey dribbling down my fur if I were to become truly intimate with the black bear as I catch the bus to work. I imagine I would be terrified by the sights and sounds of urban life. And the smells. There would be nothing inviting about the interior of the bus--or its dreaded occupants--unless the bear with whom I was truly intimate was a cute fellow, near domestication from human contact. But then my sympathetic participation in his form of life, however episodic, would be less of a step to deep ecology. A more or less tame bear is more or less the shadow of a bear.

Perhaps, though, I am to think like a bear, not in my urban environment, but in his wild one. The honey dribbling down my fur is the remains of a recent adventure. With him I remember the dense fragrance of wildflowers, sweet to the nose; somewhere, nearby, the source, hidden from the careless eye. But it was found, and, amid the buzzing protestations of the bees, we had drunk the heavy liquid, chewed the catacombed interior, and now, with honey dribbling down my fur, I am setting out in search of new satisfaction--a fish from the nearby stream, a drink from the spring.

Though not easy, this imaginary participation in a bear's life is intelligible. Because we share a common fund of experience with the black bear, we can project ourselves into his life, at least to a limited, perhaps evanescent, extent, whether we imagine ourselves as a bear in his, or in our, environment. If we have the time and inclination, we can--or so I believe--feel his pain, grow thirsty and hungry with him, take pleasure in the presence of companions, taste the honey. Our sympathetic participation in his life will--or can--make us more sensitive to his needs, less willing unthinkingly to frighten him or destroy the wilderness that is his home. Thinking like a bear, in a word, can raise our ursine consciousness. To drink honey like a bear is a step to becoming less self-centered, indeed, less species-centered, in our thinking. And it is in this respect that it is a step to deep ecology.

"Deep ecology" is the name now commonly given to a constellation of views about our proper relationship to the natural order. First introduced by the Norwegian philosopher Arne Naess,[2] the name marks the distinction between (1) views that assess the morality of our interactions with nature and its inhabitants exclusively in terms of human interests (what here will be called "anthropocentric environmental ethics" or "anthropocentrism") and (2) views that assess the morality of our interactions in ways that are not wholly anthropocentric ("nonanthropocentric environmental ethics" or "nonanthropocentrism"). Views of the former type are more or less "shallow"; those of the latter type, more or less "deep."

The more-or-less part of this contrast in many ways is as important as the basic contrast itself. In the shallow camp, for example, we find those who think that our obligations, as they involve the non-human world, are to be fixed exclusively in terms of the interests of the present generation of human beings; but we also find those who would include the interests of generations not yet born.[3] And among a view of either sort there are those who compute human interests exclusively in terms of economic criteria (for example, the criterion of willingness-to-pay), while others deny that our aesthetic and political values, for example, are reducible to units in, or are adequately reflected by, even the most refined economic theory.[4] The class of anthropocentric environmental ethics, in short, is anything but a theoretical monolith. It is home to great diversity.

The same is true of the "deep" side of the distinction. Some there are who allow the relevance of the interests of individual human beings in determining the ethics of our dealings with nature; others are openly hostile to what humans want or prefer, stridently misanthropic.[5] Some think that species as such have value, while others (often called "holists") think right and wrong are to be fixed by weighing the effects of what we do for ecosystems, possibly even the whole biosphere.[6]

We do not as yet have a full typology of the two major classes of environmental ethics--anthropocentric and non-anthropocentric. Already we know enough, however, to understand why the difference between theories belonging to the same class are no less important than their similarities. We also know why thinking like a bear is, or at least can be, a step to deep ecology. To the extent that our imagining-our-way-into-the-bear's-skin raises our ursine consciousness, makes us less species-centered in thinking about how we should act when it comes to our sometimes fatal interactions with the natural order, to that extent we are moved away from an exclusively anthropocentric environmental ethic. Not just human interests, the interests of the black bear must somehow find a place in our moral deliberation and judgment. And not only the interests of the black bear. Our imaginative penetration of the bear's way of life will not have taught us much if the lives of other, relevantly similar animals, whether domestic or wild, are ignored. If we can feel the honey dribbling down our fur, we can also taste the salt with the cow at the lick, smell the blood of the wounded caribou with the wolf, and, with the dog, hear the familiar tread of the master on the stairs.

I think any ethical theory laying claim to our rational assent must be at least this deep--must, that is, recognize the independent moral status, the direct moral relevance, of animals such as these. It is not clear how, or whether, one can "prove" that this is so; it is not clear how, or whether, one can "prove" any moral belief of this sort.[7] What one can do is consider the assumptions and implications of anthropocentrism and ask how rationally and morally satisfactory they are. For example, if a given theory considers human pain and suffering morally relevant but denies the moral relevance of the pain and suffering of the black bear, then it seems to be rationally defective. For pain is pain, and pain is in itself undesirable, to whomsoever it may occur, whether beast or human.[8] Or if a theory assumes that moral principles are the rules self-interested agents agree to have imposed on everyone's behavior, and claims that one has duties directly only to those individuals who are capable of entering into such agreements (or "contracts"), then one wants to protest, I think, that the theory's implications are morally skewed.[9] A young child, for example, lacks the abilities necessary for contracting; the theory implies, therefore, that we can do no wrong directly to the child, that we have no direct duties in this case, and so do no wrong to the child if, for example, we spend an evening's amusement torturing her. But if, as I assume, thoughtful people will agree that we owe it to the child not to torture her, despite her inability to contract, then it cannot be rational to deny that we owe it to a dog not to torture him, because he lacks the abilities required to contract. For these reasons, then, though not only for these, I do not myself believe that any version of anthropocentrism is rationally or morally satisfactory.

These sketchy objections to anthropocentric environmental ethics must face serious problems of their own. One does not offer a sound objection to a moral theory unless the objection is of a kind that is both relevant and fair. How moral theories are to be fairly and relevantly assessed, however, is a highly divisive issue, one that cannot be even superficially examined on this occasion.[10] As is always true in philosophy, questions outnumber answers. If those of us involved in this conference are to make any progress in our attempt to answer some of our questions about environmental ethics, we must assume that we can agree on how we should answer others. So let us assume, for the sake of argument--and this is a large assumption, certainly--that I am right: No version of anthropocentrism is adequate. Some form of non-anthropocentric environmental ethic, some specimen of a (more or less) deep ecology, must be where the truth lies. Our question then becomes, Which one? Or, alternatively, How deep?

One answer is: Deeper than you've gone so far. And one way to suggest the depth others would have us plumb is to recall the passage quoted at the outset. For Dogen, it will be recalled, not only became "truly intimate" with the black bear; he also "thought as a mountain." So, to understand our moral place in nature's scheme of things, the passage suggests, we must not only enter imaginatively into the lives of nonhuman animals; we must also enter imaginatively into the mute majesty of mountains--and, by implication, of oceans, stars, rocks, forests, or, in a word, all that dwells therein. To think like a black bear, on this view, is a step to deep ecology, but it is only a step, failing by itself to complete the journey of a thousand miles to the true environmental ethic.

What shall we make of the injunction to think like a mountain? Peter Singer gives part of the correct answer, I think, when he states that "such imagining yields a perfect blank."[11] Unlike the case of the black bear, with whom we share a real, even if comparatively small, family of experiences, a mountain is not a conscious individual and so has no experiences in common with us. This is why, were I to attempt to imagine being a mountain, the result would be "a perfect blank"--that is, no awareness. Thus, if, in order to demonstrate the need for an environmental ethic that is deeper than one that requires consideration of what benefits and harms nonhuman animals, we must first think the thoughts of a mountain, and given, as seems obvious, that the attempt to do this yields no thoughts at all, then the need for a deeper environmental ethic has not been demonstrated.

Singer and many others believe the lesson to be learned from this exercise is simple: the boundary of morality is sentience, where by 'sentience' is meant the capacity to experience pleasure and pain. When that capacity is present, then there is something to take into account, something of direct moral importance; when it is absent, then there is nothing of direct moral relevance to consider. Black bears are in; Black Mountain is out. Let us call this view sentientism. Is this as far, as deep, as we can or should go in our search for a nonanthropocentric environmental ethic?

If the only theory of value that required our serious consideration was one that reduces value to certain mental states or feelings, or, more particularly, if the only view of this sort worthy of our assent was hedonism (pleasant mental states have positive, painful mental stages have negative, value), then we wouldn't have a serious choice. Sentientism would win hands down. But philosophical plots are never this simple. There are important theories of value that differ from, and are inconsistent with, any unqualified version of a mental state theory, including hedonism. Of particular relevance in the present context is a view of the sort we find in Kant, where it is individuals, not their mental states, that are said to have a distinctive kind of value, what we'll call <u>inherent value</u>. Kant, it is true, offers his vision of inherent value in the course of developing a very famous anthropocentric theory,[12] so the relevance of his ideas to nonanthropocentric environmental ethical theories needs to be approached indirectly. But let us set out some of the important features of the idea of inherent value as this applies to individual human beings, as, on Kant's view, it does; then we will be able to understand what it would mean to apply this idea to those who are not human.[13]

A large part of the characterization of inherent value, or what Kant refers to as "end in itself," is negative. Among the defining characteristics are the following.

1. The inherent value of an individual human being is not reducible to, and is incommensurate with, the value of that individual's mental states. A normally happy person, for example, is not of greater inherent value than someone who is chronically depressed. Our inherent value does not wax or wane with changes in the hedonic tone of our lives.

2. The inherent value of an individual human being is not reducible to, nor does it vary with, the individual's usefulness relative to the interests of others. A surgeon, for example, has no greater inherent value, even assuming her greater utility, than a dishwasher.

3. The inherent value of an individual human being is not reducible to, nor does it vary according to the possession of, the individual's skills or other virtues, including moral virtues. Wayne Gretzky is neither more nor less inherently valuable than the substitute right wing on the company hockey team, and Mother Teresa has no greater inherent value than a woman doing time for child abuse.

4. An individual human being's inherent value is not dependent on, and is not reducible to, the attitudes and beliefs others have toward, or about, him. Those who are loved and idolized are no more valuable, inherently,

than those who are hated and despised, and persons who belong to "lower" are not less inherently valuable than those who belong to "higher" classes (e.g., Untouchables and Brahmins in India).

Though not complete, the foregoing remarks about inherent value at least should suggest how the idea offers something on which to pin our (presumed) egalitarian hopes. If, as the idea allows, all who have inherent value have it equally, then the noble vision of the equality among "all men" may have found home in theory. For differ though we do in many ways--in terms of our skills, for example, or our moral character and usefulness to others--we are all the same, all equal, when it comes to possessing this fundamental value, inherent value. Each of us is, in Kant's terminology, an end in himself or herself, and no one of us who is, is so to a lesser or greater degree than anyone else. Moreover, if this much is true, then we can glimpse both the spirit and the letter of Kant's proscription against treating one another "as means merely." This I do, for example, whenever I treat you as if your value as an individual is reducible to your usefulness to me or, less self-centeredly, to some group, even the public at large. To treat you thus is to treat you as if you were a thing, a tool, a mere resource, whose purpose for being is to advance the interests of others.

Now, types of value, like entities generally, ought not to be multiplied beyond necessity. Why, then, introduce a second, quite different kind of value (inherent value) if one kind of value (the value of mental states, such as pleasure) is enough? The short answer some philosophers give is that value of this latter kind just isn't enough. Unless our individual, equal inherent value is postulated, these thinkers believe--and Kant is one member of this group, I believe--the moral theory we will be left holding will be unequal to the task of providing a fully adequate account of moral right and wrong. In particular, such a theory will allow, possibly encourage, us to treat the individual <u>merely as a means</u> to some supposedly desirable end (for example, the general welfare). To the extent that such treatment of the individual is wrong, and assuming that any and all theories that fail to recognize our equal inherent value imply that it is not, to that extent we have good reason to deny their validity as theories and postulate our equal inherent value.

That this value is postulated in our case is not unimportant. Kant, for example, makes it abundantly clear that our value as ends-in-ourselves is not observed by the senses, nor "intuited" by the intellect in its a priori exercise. The status of inherent value in our moral theorizing, he implies, is analogous to the status of electrons in our theorizing in physics. In the latter case, we postulate that there are electrons in order both to unify and explain what we know, or what we think we know, about the physical order; analogously, then, we postulate inherent value in order to unify and explain what we know, or think we know, about the moral order. We know--or at least many of us think we know--that it is wrong to treat any human person merely as a means, regardless of race, sex, age, intellect, virtue, economic standing, etc.; and it is only by postulating our equal inherent value, or so some moral philosophers believe, that we are able to explain why this is wrong and bring unity to other, related beliefs about the wrongful treatment of the individual (for example, that it is wrong to execute a native youth known to be innocent of a crime in order to avert a race riot in the community).

The concept of inherent value, then, has important uses in anthropocentric ethical views. But it also holds promise for views that are nonanthropocentric. It has been argued, for example--and convincingly so, to my mind[14]--that possession of inherent value rationally cannot be limited only to human persons but instead must be attributed to nonhuman animals like the black bear--to animals, that is, who, like human persons, are the experiencing subjects of a life that matters to them, as individuals, independently of their usefulness to others. Indeed, the grounds for postulating inherent value in the case of these animals are the same as those we have for doing so in the case of human persons--namely, in order to unify and explain what we know, or think we know, at least on reflection, about the moral ties that bind us to these animals. Thus, though the notion of inherent value or its equivalent (e.g., Kant's concept of "end in itself") historically has been a major theme of anthropocentrism in ethics, there is no reason why it cannot play a leading role in nonanthropocentric theories.

Like sentientism, theories that are built on the notion of

inherent value ("inheritism," if this verbal barbarism will be forgiven me) can move us in the direction of a deep ecology. How deep? Here we encounter an enormously important difference between the two kinds of theory. By definition sentientism limits those individuals of direct moral concern to those who have mental states, to those who are conscious. Everything else, whether individual, group, or system, fails to possess what is of direct moral significance, so that nonsentient nature in general is consigned, in John Rodman's graphic phrase, to "the realm of thinghood."[15] Mountains, rivers, deserts, prairies, wetlands--all wilderness, wherever it may be, lacks what it takes to be of direct moral relevance. So long as we do not embrace panpsychism, everything lacking consciousness remains beyond the moral pale.

Inheritism, by contrast, is theoretically open-minded at this point. Notwithstanding the fact that theories of both human and animal rights deploy this notion, and despite the fact that both the humans and animals in question are conscious, it remains true that there is nothing in the notion of inherent value itself that necessarily limits its possession to what is capable of having mental states, to what is conscious. Anything that has a value that is not reducible to its utility for others, or to how others feel about it, or to its virtues, or to how happy or miserable it is, to that extent can have inherent value. Whether a strong case can be made for believing that it actually has such value will depend on our showing more than that these negative tests are passed, but there is nothing in the nature of these tests themselves that entails that something lacking consciousness, cannot possess value of this kind.

Once this much is seen, we should not be surprised that a variety of theories on the nonanthropocentric side affirm that a variety of things are inherently valuable. Indeed, one measure of the "depth" of nonanthropocentric theories is how much they depart from the Kantian model, where such value is limited to individual human persons (at least amongst terrestrial beings). A version of inheritism that includes individual animals like the black bear is deeper than Kant's theory, but still like it in limiting such value to individuals. A deeper theory would be one that recognized the inherent value of species as such, for example, or one that attributed such value to ecosystems, and, in either case, denied that individuals have the sort of independent value that inherent value is. The theoretical limit, perhaps, is a theory that affirms the inherent value of the biosphere itself and sees the value of the individual as mythological, a product, perhaps, of a bankrupt individualistic paradigm in Western metaphysics. If we think of the best environmental ethical theory as the key with which we open the full range of our ethical questions as these relate to the natural order, the task before us is to decide what version of nonanthropocentric theory this is, how deep we go in parting company with both the Kantian and the sentientist tradition in ethics.

How shall we rationally decide this? How can we? One way is to follow Singer and refuse to go beyond sentientism. When, in the spirit of Dogen, Singer is asked to "think like a mountain," he will find, we know, "a perfect blank" and conclude that there is nothing to consider: Since there is nothing that matters experientially to the mountain, there is nothing of direct moral importance that can matter to us. Such is the provocative ambiguity of the invitation to "think like a mountain," however, that one might reach a very different conclusion. Of course one draws a "perfect blank" when one attempts to put oneself in a mountain's shoes. Of course there is nothing that matters experientially to the mountain, nothing that gives it pleasure or causes it pain, for example. To realize these truths is, one might say, the whole point of the exercise. Well, not quite the whole point since a truth half understood is misunderstood, and the other half of the truth, the half that Singer and other sentientists fail to understand, is that we carry prejudicial baggage with us if we assume that the moral status of the mountain depends on whether it can experience anything, pleasure and pain in particular. Isn't this assumption simply an unrecognized vestige of the anthropocentrism Singer and other sentientists triumphantly think they have put behind them? For consider: A mountain doesn't have to be one of us, be human, given the sentientist's views, to be of direct moral relevance; it just has to be sufficiently like us, be sentient, to count. Isn't that so close to anthropocentrism as to make us wonder how far we've gone beyond it? To reply that one draws "a perfect blank" whenever one tries to "think like a mountain" assumes that a clear and compelling answer has been given to this question. It does not give it. It is not difficult to imagine Dogen's tolerant smile over the sentientist's treatment of this question.

I think Dogen would be right to insist on the need for more from sentientists at this juncture, and right too (if Dogen took this step) to argue that the "blank" state of mind we encounter when we "think like a mountain" is not the answer some sentientists evidently think it is. Right on both points, however, Dogenites have their work cut out for them if, short of a preemptive appeal to an unarguable mysticism, they are to move us, rationally, to a deeper environmental ethic. The need for argument is not peculiar to sentientists, so that, if, as seems to me, there is good reason to believe that standard sentientist arguments are weak,[16] it in no way follows that those who follow Dogen win by default. How, then, by way of positive argument, can an environmental ethic deeper than sentientism, deeper even than a version of inheritism that extends to the black bear and other individual animals--how can the case for a deeper theory proceed?

Among the possibilities that have been explored, three merit our attention. The first is cut from familiar theoretical cloth. Inherent value is postulated in the case of something (for example, species, ecosystems, the biosphere) to illuminate and unify our considered beliefs about right and wrong; theories that attempt to avoid postulating inherent value, we are to suppose, fail to offer the desirable illumination and unity. By way of example: Some have argued[17] that species *as such* must be viewed as having inherent value because (a) thoughtful people agree that it is wrong to render any species extinct and because (b) the only satisfactory way to account for this belief is by postulating independent, inherent value for species in and of themselves.

This approach cannot be any stronger than the success proponents have in convincing us that both (a) and (b) are true. Success is not easy to come by in either case. Although many people are enthusiastic about the immorality of destroying some species (for example, the great blue whale, the African elephant, and the Siberian tiger), moral vigor wanes in the case of obscure species of plant or species of lethal viruses. Comparatively few people are of the opinion that we would do something wrong if we killed the last four remaining specimens of _Phacelia argilaceae_ (all of which are enclosed by a fence in an inhospitable region of Utah), and even fewer believe it would be wrong to destroy, absolutely, every trace of the smallpox virus (_Poxvirus variolae_); most people, it seems, would happily consign that species to utter oblivion. So it is, at best, an unstable platform, this attempt to argue for the inherent value of species as such because otherwise we will be unable to unify and illuminate the moral beliefs thoughtful people have about the extinction of species. Whether right or wrong, most people, even thoughtful ones, seem to be selective when it comes to the species they think ought to be saved.

Or consider variations of the so-called "last man argument."[18] You are the last human being on earth. None will come after you, and you know it. You have the means to blow the earth to smithereens before you die; or you can leave it be, to work out its future destiny on its own, so to speak. What ought you to do? Some there are who think that thoughtful people will speak with one voice: Don't blow it up. There is room for robust skepticism on this point, however, and a skepticism that is dwarfed by the one that surrounds the suggestion that the only or best way to account for this presumed belief about the desirability of saving the earth is by attributing inherent value to it. Equally plausible, it seems, is the suggestion that destroying it when this is avoidable would be surprisingly ungrateful, like smashing the dinner plates after the host has dropped dead of a heart attack. Just as I owe the host, even when deceased, behavior that displays my thanks for the opportunity to dine, so I owe the earth something like a debt of gratitude for my past life. Or so it may be argued. It is more in the nature of a leap of faith than a reasoned argument to conclude that we must attribute inherent value to the earth if we are to have any reason, as the last man, not to blow it to kingdom come.

A second possibility for deeper theories is to resurrect naturalism in ethics. Where we find certain facts (for example, facts of the form X-is-alive), there we also find values (of the form, say, x-is-inherently-good), and, once values take up independent lodging in the world, obligation cannot be far behind. From "X is inherently good" more than a few have derived "X ought not to be destroyed." But naturalism is a vision ill-suited to the dominant temper of the times, where the shadows of both Hume and Moore are still cast across the thought of most of their philosophical descendants. Even in the case of the most promising work among the new naturalists--Paul Taylor's ethic of respect for nature[19]--the centuries old doubts do not go away. With Taylor we can, I think, agree that living things are teleological centers of life, all "striving" to realize their individual potential--their good, if you like, a good they have independently of their usefulness to us. But the good we find here seems an inadequate sort of good on which to erect human obligations. An oak tree that fully actualizes its natural propensities is, let us agree, a better oak tree than one that does not--is better as an oak tree, better of its kind. That something is good-of-its-kind, however, creates no obligation to preserve or protect it. Otherwise we would be obliged to rally round and save Henry Lee Lucas, who, as the confessed murderer of over 150 people, is the best of his kind, the most prolific murderer, we have yet encountered. If, in reply, we are told that it is exemplars of natural kinds that we are to preserve and protect, the case seems just as counter intuitive. A specimen of bella donna is good of its kind if it has the power to kill off the unwary hiker. Must we, therefore, act to save the most virulent strains, out of respect for their value? I do not think it unfair to give a negative answer to this question in particular and to resist in general the suggestion that living things that are good of their kind ought to be respected and preserved. This sort of goodness (good of its kind), which is, I think, naturalistic, is not equal to the theoretical task of grounding human obligations. Morally significant values, ones on which our duties are based, are not facts in the way naturalism assumes or requires. Or so it seems to me.

The third possibility worthy of consideration has mystical markings. Rooted in the awareness of the interconnectedness of all things (my body, for example, in all likelihood contains atoms from a long dead brontosauras, from an even older dead star, from the body of Julius Ceasar)--rooted in this awareness, a mystical environmental ethic transports us beyond the illusoriness of separateness, including the myth of the separateness of our own individual being, and replaces this pedestrian vision of the self and world with a more or less ineffable vision of the unity or sameness of all that is. Where before we took comfort in the ignorant sound of two hands clapping, we now listen to the wise timbre of the solitary hand.

It would be nice--or so many will suppose--if unbridled monism could be summarily dismissed. But it is both too old and too new for that, and the names and life-ways associated are too noble to allow a breezy rejection to count. "Merely to list the variations on (the) theme," writes Theodore Roszak,[20] himself an ardent supporter, "would fill a book. Lao Tzu teaching 'the great Tao flows everywhere'...the Vedic wisdom which can say of all things the eye may light upon 'tat tuam asi'--that's you!...the Avatamsaka Sutra that transfigures the universe into the Buddha's sacred body of light...the night Hermetic Uroborus inscribed 'One is All'...the Wakan-Tanka of the American Indians, whose presence made every object holy, as much the stone as man...Blake summoning us 'To see a world in a grain of sand'...Dylan Thomas discovering that 'The force that through the green fuse drives the flower drives my blood'..." A recent addition to this list, John Seed, the Australian environmentalist, expresses the unitary vision in these terms.[21]

When humans investigate and see through their layers of anthropocentric self-cherishing, a most profound change in consciousness begins to take place.

Alienation subsides. The human is no longer an outsider, apart. Your humaneness is then recognized as being merely the most recent stage of your existence, and as you stop identifying exclusively with this chapter, you start to get in touch with yourself as mammal, as vertebrate, as a species only recently emerged from the rain forest. As the fog of amnesia disperses, there is a transformation in your relationship to other species, and in your commitment to them... "I am protecting the rain forest" develops into "I am the part of the rain forest recently emerged into thinking." What a relief then: The thousands of years of (imagined) separation are over and we begin to recall our true nature. That is, the change is a spiritual one, thinking like a mountain, sometimes referred to as deep ecology.

As your memory improves, as the implications of the sciences of evolution and ecology are internalised and replace the outmoded anthropocentric structures in your mind, there is identification with all life. There follows the realisation that the distinction between 'life' and 'lifeless' is a human construct. Every atom in this body existed before organic life emerged 4,000 million years ago. Remember your own childhood as minerals, as lava, as rocks? Rocks contain the potentiality to weave themselves into such stuff as this. We are the rocks dancing. Why do we look down on them with such a condescending air? It is they that are the immortal part of us.

It is hard to decide what to say of the stuff of which the unitary vision is made. It is tempting to dismiss it, not because the arguments are bad (more often than not, there are no arguments, good or bad), but because most of it is unintelligible to the outsider. On the other hand, it is tempting to be tempted, to give in to the pull of union-with-nature which, I assume, all of us feel at times in our life. (I do, in any event.) If the power and existence of the feeling were the marks of its truth, we would know where to stand. But feelings, alas, do not wear their veracity on their sleeves, so that we must, if we are to show respect for the ordinary canons of reason, think about, not merely experience, the unitary vision, test its mettle by critical reflection, not accept its validity on the grounds that it is psychologically compelling or because ancient sages and noble peoples have believed it. And here's the rub. For the noble vision does not fare well when subjected to tests which, administered in other quarters to other views, are fair.

For example: There are problems enough in making sense of my identity over time as a human person, if we accept a worldview that has human persons in it. How much more difficult must it be, therefore, to tie my identity to the rain forest or to 4 billion year old atoms. What can be the criterion of identity, given such a view? If I am the same as a rock because we both contain some of the same atoms of a more ancient bit of matter, what is it that makes this atom, now, the same as the atom it was then? I do not think we have any easy, or possibly any intelligible, answers ready to hand. It is not clear to me whether, in the end, it is the

sound rather than the substance of the ideas that attracts us--
their novelty, their psychological resonance, their romance.
But not their truth.

Most proponents of the unitary vision are not unaware of the
difficulties others find; nor are they short on replies. The
limits of both time and my own knowledge make it impossible
for me even to attempt to do justice to this debate here. The
perennial philosophy does not lend itself to simple confir-
mation. Or disconfirmation. (Or, possibly, to neither!) I hope
it is not unfair to note, however, that the gaze of the unitary
vision seems not so much to avoid, as to raise to a different
environment, the problems that plague more pedestrian accounts
of the world and our place in it. If, for example, naturalism
is not a credible theory of value given our ordinary, non-
unitary vision, it is difficult to understand how the case is
any different if, in place of natural facts, we have mystical
ones. It is, that is, not clear to me how we can infer that
something _is good_, in any morally significant sense of "good,"
simply from our knowledge or realization that something _is_.
If, in reply, we are told that mystical knowledge of value is
immediate, not inferential, so that in knowing the true nature
of what is we also know, immediately, the truth about what is
good and ought to be, then we ought, I think, to test this ice
very carefully before skating on it. To advance a position
that builds in its own immunity from criticism runs the risk of
permitting nonsense to pass for truth. And the greater the
possible truth, the greater the actual risk.

Some will view this reluctance to take such a risk as a
symptom of a deeper, more sinister uneducability. George
Sessions, whose influential work I commend to your attention,
may have this in mind when he voices his "fear that many
Western philosophers and other intellectuals are so thoroughly
entrenched in their Western academic training and methodologies
and narrow specialties that they are going to be of very little
help toward, and might actually constitute a reactionary
hindrance to, the development of an ecological paradigm"[22] of
the sort we find articulated, for example, by John Seed. Well,
perhaps. But perhaps these "reactionaries," if not on the side
of the angels, at least are on the side of what is true. The
veracity of the unitary vision, the "new ecological paradigm,"
if accepted by enough of us, would move us to an environ-

mental ethic deeper than the one I would personally endorse, the one that knows the feel and taste of honey dribbling down our fur. To go any deeper than this, to my mind at least, is to get in way over our heads when we can, and rationally should, avoid it.

North Carolina State University

NOTES

1. Robert Aitken, Roshi "Gandhi, Dogen and Deep Ecology," quoted by John Seed, "Anthropocentrism Questioned," *Ecophilosophy V,* George Sessions and Bill Devall, eds., p. 14.

2. Arne Naess, "The Shallow and the Deep Long-Range Ecology Movements," *Inquiry,* vol. 16 (1973), pp. 95-100.

3. As representative of the former view, see Gregory Kavka, "The Futurity Problem," in R.I. Sikora and Brian Barry, eds., *Obligations to Future Generations* (Philadelphia: Temple University Press, 1978), pp. 186-203. The latter position finds expression in, for example, Annette Baier, "For the Sake of Future Generations," in Tom Regan, ed., *Earthbound: New Introductory Essays in Environmental Ethics* (New York: Random House, 1983.) Additional references are found in Baier's "Suggestions for Further Reading."

4. As representative of the former view, see William Baxter, *People or Penguins: The Case for Optimal Pollution* (New York: Columbia University Press, 1974). The latter position finds expression in, for example, Mark Sagoff, "Ethics and Economics in Environmental Law," in Tom Regan, ed., *Earthbound, op. cit.* Additional references are found in Sagoff's "Suggestions for Further Reading."

5. As representative of the former view, see William Aiken, "Ethical Issues in Agriculture," in Tom Regan, ed., *Earthbound, op. cit.* (The latter position finds expression in, for example, J. Baird Callicott, "Animal Liberation: A Triangular Affair,") *Environmental Ethics* 2, no. 4 (Winter 1980), pp. 311-38. Additional references are found in Sagoff's "Suggestions For Further Reading."

6. As representative of the former view, see Alastaire Gunn, "Why Preserve Rare Species?" in Tom Regan, ed., *Earthbound, op. cit.* The latter position finds expression in, for example, Callicott's "Animal Liberation: A Triangular Affair," *op. cit.* Additional references are found in Gunn's "Suggestions for Further Reading."

7. These issues are pursued more fully in my *The Case For Animal Rights* (Berkeley: University of California Press, 1983) Chapter 4.

8. The point is made forcefully by both Bentham and Mill, for example. See their respective selections in Tom Regan and Peter Singer, eds., *Animal Rights and Human Obligations* (Englewood Cliffs: Prentice-Hall, 1976).

9. The point is pursued at length in my *The Case for Animal Rights, op. cit.,* Chapter 5.

10. See *The Case For Animal Rights,* Chapter 4, for a discussion of these issues.

11. Peter Singer, *Practical Ethics* (New York: Oxford University Press, 1982) p. 92. Singer refers to a weed, not a mountain, in the passage cited. The philosophical point remains the same.

12. See, for example, Immanuel Kant, *The Fundamental Principles of the Metaphysic of Morals,* many editions.

13. A fuller discussion is offered in Chapter 7 of *The Case For Animal Rights, op. cit.*

14. *Ibid.*

15. John Rodman, "The Liberation of Nature," *Inquiry,* 20 (1977), pp. 83-131.

16. I argue this in, for example, "The Nature and Possibility of an Environmental Ethic," *Environmental Ethics,* 3 (1981), pp. 19-34; reprinted in Tom Regan, *All That Dwell Therein: Essays on Animal Rights and Environmental Ethics* (Berkeley: University of California Press, 1982) pp. 184-205.

17. See, for example, the essay by Callicott cited above.

18. For a full discussion, see Robert Elliot, *An Environmental Ethic* (Ph.D. Dissertation, Queensland University).

19. Paul Taylor, "The Ethics of Respect for Nature," *Environmental Ethics,* 3, no. 3, 1981. Taylor's views are much deeper and more subtle than I am able to suggest here.

20. Theodore Rozak, *Where the Wasteland Ends* (New York: Doubleday Books, 1973) p. 398.

21. John Seed, "Anthropocentrism Questioned," in George Sessions and Bill Devall, eds., *Ecophilosophy* V, pp. 11-12.

22. George Sessions, *ibid.,* p. 7. Sessions' address is Sierra College, Rocklin, California, 95677.

THE EVOLVING ANTITRUST REGULATION OF THE PROFESSIONS

Maura A. O'Brien

The Federal Trade Commission (FTC) has recently fought a heated legislative battle to maintain jurisdiction over the antitrust activities of the professions, and to supervene state laws which permit or encourage restrictive trade practices in these groups (American Medical Association v. FTC on writ of certiorari of the U.S. Court of Appeals of the 2d Cir., March 23, 1982). This battle is not the first of its kind. Challenges of government regulation have arisen since the Sherman Antitrust Act of 1890 was first viewed in relation to the professions. The authority of the Sherman Act was initially construed to forbid: (1) contracts, combinations or conspiracies in restraint of trade, and (2) all monopolistic practices.[1] The antitrust laws, whose basic premise is that competition will produce lower prices in addition to better goods and services, were originally not applied to the professions due to their ethical and public commitments.

The Supreme Court acknowledged that the public service aspect of a profession distinguished it from a business yet, despite this distinction, failed to justify an antitrust exemption for the professions. The antitrust goal of economic efficiency and unrestrained competition remained constant yet the methods of antitrust analysis were unclear and failed to provide guidance to determine the illegality of conduct.

The evolution of law demonstrates that the key issue today is not whether professions are, or should be, exempt from antitrust scrutiny. The question is, given that they are not exempt, which methodology should be chosen to determine whether violations have, in fact, occurred? If "special treatment" is indeed to be given to the professions, their ethical principles must receive equal recognition and consideration before the assignment of appropriate weights by the judiciary. If the policy of economic efficiency is to remain supreme, the existence of competing ethical principles demands the moral justification of its precedence. By developing the restrictive rule of reason method to constitute "special treatment," the Court failed in both tasks.

I. The Nature of a Profession

· The term "profession" has traditionally been applied to the learned professions of medicine, law and theology. Leon Kass, M.D. asserts the following:
> Medicine, despite technological advances and societal changes, remains essentially what it has always been; a profession rather than a trade, with its own ends, means, and intrinsic norms of conduct. Being a professional is an ethical matter, entailing devotion to a way of life, in the service of others and of some higher good.[2]

This traditional outlook was one which was used as the basis for the decision rendered in U.S. v. Oregon State Medical Society (343 US 236 (1952)) from which the following is excerpted:
> ...there are ethical considerations where the historic direct relationship between patient and physician is involved which are quite different from the usual considerations prevailing in ordinary commercial matters. (Id. at 246)

In this case, the Court upheld the Oregon physicians who established the Blue Shield programs as an anticompetitive measure designed to discourage independent health plans. Although the Court did not specify whether an exemption existed for the other "learned professions," it applied the ethical considerations of the doctor-patient relationship broadly which enabled the Court to conclude that the usual forms of business competition could be "demoralizing to the ethical standards of a profession" (346 US at 336). Although the actions of the Oregon physicians were designed to be anticompetitive and did restrain trade in violation of the Sherman Act, the Court chose not to apply the antitrust laws because of an overriding, yet undefined, ethical principle intrinsic to the doctor-patient relationship. The Oregon State Medical Society decision discouraged antitrust attacks for more than two decades; it was not until 1975, in Goldfarb v. Virginia State Bar, that the exemption of the professions was challenged.

II. Goldfarb v. Virginia State Bar

At issue in Goldfarb v. Virginia State Bar (421 US 773 (1975)) was the legality of a minimum fee schedule for real

estate closings established by a local bar association. The Supreme Court, upon a reinterpretation of the Sherman Act, held that the policy of economic efficiency upon which the Act is based is meant to extend broadly to groups which act in a primarily economic fashion; the nature of an occupation, standing alone, does not provide sanctuary from the Sherman Act. The Court denied that professions were exempt from antitrust jurisdiction yet felt compelled, in its famous footnote 17, to acknowledge that professions do differ from businesses:
> The fact that a restraint operates upon a profession as distinguished from a business is, of course, relevant in determining whether that particular restraint violates the Sherman Act. It would be unrealistic to view the practice of professions as interchangeable with other business activities, and automatically to apply to the professions antitrust concepts which originated in other areas. The public service aspect, and other features of the profession, may require that a particular practice, which could properly be viewed as a violation of the Sherman Act in another context, be treated differently. We intimate no view on any other situation than the one with which we are confronted today. (421 US at 788-9 n. 17)

This ambiguity of the Court's statement could support the interpretation that a special treatment of professionals is warranted in cases in which its "public service" aspect is cited as justification for the anticompetitive action. Although the language in Goldfarb suggests that some differentiation may be drawn between a "profession" and a "business," the Court has never relied upon such a distinction in upholding the legality of professional conduct.[3] These strong hints of the Court that professions do differ from commercial enterprises in some respects, and therefore may merit a more thorough-going review, left the door open for special treatment of the professionals in certain cases.

The outcome of the Goldfarb decision (421 US 773 (1975)) was twofold: (1) The Court clarified that professionals do not enjoy a broad antitrust exemption, yet (2) the Court did not clarify what constituted "special treatment" of the professions and when it was to be conducted. The court implied that an argument of principle, based on the unique public service aspect of a profession, was overruled by the policy consideration with which it competed. The possibility that an argument of principle may be relevant, as revealed in footnote 17, demonstrated a need for a systematic method of judicial analysis to determine the illegality of alleged antitrust violations by professionals. It was necessary that this method acknowledge and consider the public service element mentioned in Goldfarb to enable the Court to specify which considerations, if any, are possible counterweights to antitrust activity.

III. Statute Interpretation: Per Se and Rule of Reason Analysis

In addition to the lack of guidance to secure the goals of antitrust, the Sherman Act failed to delineate how courts should determine which restraints are "illegal." The statute literally bans all "restraints of trade" yet since every commercial agreement restrains trade to some extent, a distinction between reasonable restraints and undue restraints was necessary. As the courts became familiar with varying restraints in different commercial contexts, judicial interpretation of the statute gradually yielded two types of antitrust analysis: (1) agreements whose nature is so plainly anticompetitive that no extensive study is needed to establish their illegality as "per se" illegal; and (2) agreements whose competitive effect can only be evaluated by analyzing the facts peculiar to the business, the history of the restraint, and the reasons why it was imposed. The latter agreements are examined under a "rule of reason" analysis.[4]

In both methods of analysis, the Court sought to invalidate activities which were detrimental to competition and which were antagonistic to the policy of economic efficiency. The Court did not construct a theory of political rights granted by the legislature in enacting the Sherman Act; however, it did construct a policy argument to justify the enactment of the statute. Although these two analyses provide a policy guideline for determining the illegality of alleged antitrust violations, they did not specify which considerations or principles, if any, would be regarded as possible counterweights to the anticompetitive nature of the restraint.

IV. National Society of Professional Engineers v. United States

In National Society of Professional Engineers (NSPE) v. United States (435 US 679 (1978)), the Supreme Court examined a section of the NSPE canon of ethics that prohibited members from submitting competitive bids for engineering services. The NSPE attempted to justify this canon by maintaining that competitive regulation would produce inferior engineering work and thereby endanger public health and safety.

The Court did refer to the Goldfarb decision when reasserting that "by their nature, professional services may differ significantly from other business services and, accordingly, the nature of competition in such services may vary."[5] Justice Stevens, in the majority opinion in the Professional Engineers case, noted that competition and the ethical principles of the profession may indeed conflict:

> The Court is faced with the contention that a total ban on competitive bidding is necessary because otherwise engineers will be tempted to submit deceptively low bids.... The equation of competition with deception is simply too broad; we may assume that competition is not entirely conducive to ethical behavior, but that is not a reason, cognizable under the Sherman Act, for doing away with competition.[6]

Justice Blackmun, in a separate but concurring opinion revealed the difficulties inherent in the rule of reason approach and its inadequacy as a method of antitrust analysis for cases concerning the professions:

> My skepticism about going further in this case by shaping the rule of reason to such a narrow list as does the majority[7] arises from the fact that there may be ethical rules which have a more than de minimis anticompetitive effect and yet are important in a profession's proper ordering....In acknowledging that "professional services may differ significantly from other business services" and that the "nature of the competition in such services may vary," (Goldfarb v. Virginia State Bar, 421 US at 788-9, n. 17 (1975)), but then holding that ethical norms can pass muster under the rule of reason only if they promote competition, I am not at all certain that the Court leaves

enough elbow room for a realistic application of the Sherman Act to professional services.[8]

These difficulties noted in the Professional Engineers decision have not prevented the rule of reason analysis from being used as the definitive method to determine the illegality of antitrust violations by professionals. The primacy of economic competition implicit in the Sherman Act, as interpreted by the Court, has sustained its reliability as a measure of the procompetitive consequences of an alleged restraint. The unacceptability of the unchallenged assertion that this policy reigns supreme stems from a disregard for competing ethical principles, and from the failure to morally justify the primacy of the policy according to any philosophical theory.

V. Philosophical Principles and Antitrust Regulation

The basis of antitrust law is economic efficiency; therefore, the debate concerning the regulation of the professions ensues when the philosophical principles (or public service aspect of the profession) conflict with the economic policy espoused by the Sherman Act. According to the theory to which one subscribes, a judge should recognize and consider the concepts of liberty, utility or wealth maximization before rendering an interpretative judgment in which a principle or a policy (in this case, economic efficiency) takes precedence. The positions of libertarianism, utilitarianism and wealth maximization represent the competing ethical principles which conflict with the Sherman Act's goal of economic efficiency. A normative basis of antitrust law cannot be grounded on any of these three positions and, when the law conflicts with these principles, the three positions are not considered as equal counterweights. In fact, the rationale for antitrust legislation may actually hinder the securement of liberty, utility or wealth maximization.

After discussing the three aforementioned theories, it is argued that the proper role of the court (to render interpretative judgments) is not presently fulfilled in antitrust cases concerning the professions. The Supreme Court has consistently made interpretative judgments but the rule of reason analysis, by excluding the consideration of the philosophical principles without procompetitive benefits, unjustifiably narrowed the scope of interpretation. The principles and policies were not considered with equal concern before the assignment of priorities. Instead, the primacy of the policy of economic efficiency was an assumption in force since the enactment of the Sherman Act, and has been consistently used to measure (and to often exclude) the worth of the competing principles of the profession, even though the existence of such principles according to the Court, warranted the "special treatment" of the professions.

A. Liberty

The libertarian position would not attack the antitrust regulation of the professions with such vehemence if the goal of antitrust laws was to ensure that men are free to compete (or not) unrestrained by the use of force. The libertarian views the current antitrust regulation as a system of arbitrary dictation and ex post facto rulings which encourages the practices it seeks to regulate:

> We can attack artificial conditions, but are impotent when opposing natural conditions....America has hitherto pursued the exactly reverse methods, blaming economic forces tending to concentrate industry, and joining issue by means of antitrust legislation, a series of entirely artificial measures....The results have been pitiful--violent restriction of fruitful initiative....[The legislation] does not touch the rest of the evil, (it) enlarges, in place of restraining, artificial conditions, and finally regulates and complicates matters whose supreme needs are simplification and removal of restrictions.[9]

Based on the libertarian's assumption that business "always tends to adopt those practices and that scale of activity which maximize profits and incomes and serve the consumer best,[10] any harassment of business practice by government can only hamper business efficiency and reward inefficiency.[11] The vagueness of antitrust laws further complicates the issue. The restraint's criterion of "substantially lessening competition" implicitly assumes that competition is some sort of quantity. The libertarian position is based on the view that competition is a "process" whereby individuals and firms supply goods on the market without using force. The Sherman Act's emphasis on "collusion in restraint of trade" implies that it is necessary to place limitations on the liberty of the participants (i.e. the destruction of cooperation in cartels and monopolies) to maintain competition.

This compulsory competition and banned cooperation is incompatible with the "free market" system supported by libertarians due to their belief that a restriction of liberty cannot be justified when it would result in inefficiency and lower productivity. Since most libertarians would regard a cartel as "the voluntary pooling of assets in one firm to serve the consumers efficiently,"[12] they maintain that the antimonopolists must then advocate the destruction of corporations, partnerships or mergers which serve the same purposes. The government's move to prohibit practices which restrain trade is, according to the libertarian view, a restraint in itself:

...and all it can do is to impose restrictions which may issue in monopoly, when they go so far as to require permission for the individual to engage in production. This is the essence of the Society-of-Status. The reversion to status law in the antitrust legislation went unnoticed...the politicians...had secured a law under which it was impossible for the citizen to know beforehand what constituted a crime, and which therefore made all productive effort liable to prosecution if not to certain conviction.[13]

B. Utility

Utility, like the principle of liberty, is not the basis of reasoning for the antitrust regulation of professional activity. Utilitarianism, as a normative theory of law, holds that the moral worth of a law is to be judged by its effect in promoting happiness--or a determined "good"--aggregated across all of the inhabitants of society.[14] According to the utilitarian position, law is right or good if it maximizes happiness thereby enabling individuals to satisfy their preferences. A theory of rights in itself carries no import; rights in a utilitarian system are viewed only as instrumental goods. If the final good could be maximized by limiting or even disregarding the rights of individuals, then the act which promotes this good is justified.

The antitrust regulation of the professions could be defended on utilitarian grounds if the prohibition of restrictive trade practices and monopolies increased the aggregate sum of happiness or "good" in society. Yet the efficiency underlying antitrust regulation does not necessarily promote happiness. If the antitrust goal of economic efficiency is achieved, which has not been demonstrated, the limitation of personal and professional autonomy still results in a "disutility" for individuals concerned. The very nature of regulation implies that an external mechanism is essential to promote or prohibit a certain type of practice that otherwise would not result, and therefore represents a disutility to the individual who would have acted in different fashion without the constraint.

C. Wealth Maximization

Richard Posner defines the economic analysis of law in normative terms as the maximization or the enhancement of wealth. According to his view, the role of the judiciary in the "hypothetical" market is to make an interpretative judgment by determining the value or economic worth of the relevant act (or distribution of goods). The judge, therefore, should render a decision which increases the amount of wealth in the specific situation. A distribution of rights consistent with the goal of wealth maximization may be altered by market functions and legal rules.

Wealth maximization as an ethical principle, like liberty and utility, cannot be used to justify the goal or methodology of antitrust law; free markets, although perhaps inequitable, tend to maximize the wealth of society. The imposition of constraints by regulation, although aimed at the promotion of economic efficiency, does not necessarily maximize wealth. The former goal could be achieved by the destruction of monopolies which, in actuality, may preclude the latter goal. Efficiency cannot be equated with the maximization of wealth; the definition of efficiency is that of an effective operation as measured by a comparison of production and cost. By viewing cost in relation to production, an efficient practice may encourage, but does not entail, wealth maximization. Wealth maximization may, in some cases, be a by-product of antitrust regulation but, like the principles of liberty and utility it does not provide a rationale for such regulation.

D. Economic Efficiency

Antitrust regulation focuses on the policy of economic efficiency yet the Court, in basing decisions upon an interpretation of the Sherman Act, does not attempt to morally justify economic efficiency as a goal or to assert and defend the moral foundations of efficiency. This is precisely the problem. The role of the judiciary is to render a "fair" decision based on the particulars of a case. A policy cannot be assumed to be morally justified (and subsequent decisions therefore "fair") when it clashes with ethical principles whose competing claims are not specifically addressed. The goal of unrestrained competition posited by the Sherman Act was assumed to be the promotion of economic efficiency. Although there is nothing intrinsically wrong with this concept, problems ensue when market intervention and a restriction of liberty are deemed necessary to achieve this goal. Although the economic justification of unrestrained competition is apparent, a moral justification of the supremacy of this policy, especially when challenged by competing ethical principles, is warranted but never posited.

It is evident from the discussion in this section that the policy of economic efficiency cannot be justified by the libertarian, utilitarian or wealth maximization positions. Antitrust regulation intervenes in a "free" market thereby restricting the liberty of the producer to engage in certain practices or activities and the liberty of the consumer to purchase or benefit from such practices. The economic justification of such action is an appeal to the pursuit of economic efficiency. Whether or not a well regulated market operates more efficiently than a free market is beyond the scope of this paper. However, the regulation of activities (of professions) which are distinguished by ethical considerations warrants a moral, and not merely an economic, justification when a judicial decision fails to weigh, or perhaps overrides without considering, these competing principles.

VI. Conclusion

Antitrust activity, in the Court's view, may be conducted for one of two purposes: (1) a procompetitive goal, prefaced in the public service aspect or ethical norms of a profession, focuses on an outcome such as the protection of small business, the safety of the community, and enhancement in the quality of services, or a decrease in prices; and (2) an anticompetitive activity, designed to discourage competitive practice, primarily seeks to impede arrangements that would stimulate competition. By defining antitrust activity as such, the Court's consideration of the public service aspect of the professions focused only on its procompetitive goals. This can be criticized for two reasons: (a) If the defense could demonstrate that these procompetitive goals did exist, the Court was not equipped with a mechanism for weighing and ranking the priorities of the arguments of ethical principle and of economic policy. The Court, in the decisions previously discussed, has consistently chosen to give priority to the latter; (b) The rule of reason's limitation to the procompetitive goals of a restraint fails to consider cases where anticompetitive acts did not perform a competitive function but did have other public service benefits.

The Court has consistently recognized the ethical distinction of the professions but has failed to grant equal consideration. The Court has not determined the existence of a need to defend or to morally justify the policy espoused by the Sherman Act. Whether or not this is the proper function of the judiciary is not addressed in this paper. However, when cases regarding professions arise in which the competing principles warrant "special treatment" for these groups, it is no longer possible to assume that a previously unchallenged policy is supreme. Special treatment, in this case, is never clearly outlined by the Court. If such treatment is to be developed rather than to remain a continual source of allusion, it is necessary to recognize and to weigh the competing principles and policies before determining the assignment of appropriate weights. The development of the narrow rule of reason analysis, which constituted "special treatment" according to the Court, is an insufficient mechanism to achieve this purpose.

Kennedy Institute of Ethics

NOTES

1. Edmund D. Pellegrino, "What is a Profession? The Ethical Implications of the FTC Order and Some Supreme Court Decisions," Speech for the 21st Annual Residents Conference and Alumni Weekend (Washington, D.C.: Department of Opthamology, June 11, 1983), p. 3.

2. Leon R. Kass, "Professing Ethically: On the Place of Ethics in Defining Medicine," *JAMA,* Volume 249, No. 10, March 11, 1983, p. 1305.

3. Robert F. Leibenluft and Michael R. Pollard, "Antitrust Scrutiny of the Health Professions: Developing a Framework for Assessing Private Restraints," *Vanderbilt Law Review,* Volume 34, No. 849, Spring, 1981, p. 943.

4. Leibenluft and Pollard, pp. 936-7.

5. *NSPE v. US,* 696 citing with approval *Goldfarb v. Virginia State Bar* (421 US 773 (1978) n. 17).

6. *NSPE v. US* (435 US 679 696 (1978)).

7. The Court has not always applied the rule of reason with such rigor even to commercial businesses. See *Appalachian Coals, Inc. v. United States* (288 US 344, 77 L Ed 825, 53 S Ct 471 (1933)); *Chicago Board of Trade v. U.S.* (246 US 231, 62 L ED 683, 38 S Ct 242 (1918)).

8. Id. at 699.

9. Paul de Rousiers, *Les Industrires Monopolisees aux Etats-Unis,* as quoted in Gustave de Molinari, *The Society of Tomorrow* (New York: G.P. Putnam's Sons, 1904), p. 194.

10. Murray Rothbard, *Power and Market* (Kansas City, Mo.: Sneed Andrews & McNeel, Inc., 1970), p. 60.

11. See John W. Scoville and Noel Sargent, *Fact and Fancy in the TNEC Monographs* (New York: National Association of Manufacturers, 1942), pp. 298-321, 671-74.

12. Rothbard, p. 61.

13. Isabel Paterson, *The God of the Machine* (New York: G.P. Putnam's Sons, 1943), pp. 176-77.

14. Richard A. Posner, "Utilitarianism, Economics, and Legal Theory," *The Journal of Legal Studies,* Volume 8, No. 103, January, 1979, p. 104.

LIMITS ON THE STANDARDS OF PRIVATE ASSOCIATIONS

John Snapper

It is apparent that associations consisting of professionals are well equipped to deal with new issues arising from changing technologies.[1] In the early 1930's, the government through the National Industrial Redevelopment Act, formally recognized the expertise of private assocations and authorized many associations to set industrial standards. Since then, however, the mood in this country has been opposed to regulation through private association. Anti-trust law has been widely used to prevent associations from setting standards. In keeping with the current legal attitude, I argue here for severe limits on the power of private associations to set standards.

I make two claims. First, we should recognize as valid any appeal of any association rule to the civil courts. That holds for even such trivial matters as the dues level of a professional association. That is, I think that court jurisdiction over association rules ought to hold in general, even when there is no particular statute (such as the anti-trust law) against which to test the rules. I expect that few would bother to question their dues in court and that most courts would either refuse to admit jurisdiction or laughingly uphold them. But I argue that even these trivial things (and I can imagine cases where dues levels are not trivial) are the valid concern of the courts. Secondly I argue that certain sorts of matters are specially the province of state law and that no private associations should set standards for their membership concerning them without explicitly qualified prior state authorization. These matters include some of those areas in which professionals have special expertise and for which professional societies have indeed attempted to set standards for themselves.

The claim that association standards ought to be subject to judicial review is not in itself very controversial. It is hard to imagine a code of conduct of the sort discussed in this paper that would not face challenge under the particular statutes of anti-trust law. Since the point of even the self-imposition of a standard is to influence business practice and business practice is the concern of anti-trust law, any such standard may be scrutinized under that law. But I argue more generally here for court review outside of the context of the anti-trust law. If my arguments were accepted, the state authority over the standards of private associations would not depend on any particular statutes such as comprise anti-trust law, but would follow from a more general theory of what is the proper concern of professional associations and of the state.

#1. A Case History

As an example of a need for new professional standards arising out of changing technology, I will look at attempts to provide standards for design innovation. It is a common view that inventors should have some rights over their innovations and that it is wrong to simply copy others' designs. This implies standards for what counts as innovative design and what counts as a copy of an innovation. The law of property has developed over the last few centuries a doctrine under which claims to intellectual property must, for the most part, take the form of patents or copyrights. There are established criteria for granting patents and copyrights that include guidelines for what counts as an original design. However as innovative technology changes the notion of invention and discovery, it is very possible that the criteria for patent and copyright protection no longer apply with ease. Intellectual property standards are presently controversial since such a change is taking place as inventors make more creative use of computerized processes. Since computer technology makes traditional legal criteria obsolete, there are apparently now inadequate protections for computerized innovations. At issue here will then be what professional associations can do to provide standards that fill the gap in the present legal picture.

The unhappy situation is that innovations which appear as computer programs look sufficiently different from traditional innovation that they are poorly protected by either patent or copyright under present standards. In a series of cases culminating in <u>Diamond v. Diehr</u>,[2] the Supreme Court has asserted that patent protection is inapplicable to computer software. The argument is that a computational method resembles a mathematical algorithm, and by established standards for patents, no mathematical discovery is patentable. Although in Diehr, the Court did allow a patent, the Court only did this by viewing the software at issue as part of a more complex mechanized procedure. Even so the Court was deeply split over the case and did reiterate its general dislike of patents on software. Partly in response to the lack of patent protection, software innovators have turned to copyright protection. Recently, in Franklin v. Apple,[3] the courts have indicated their willingness to grant these protections. The cases, however, still await Supreme Court decisions, and this author, at least, has extreme doubts about the usefulness of this sort of protection. The point here is that copyrights only protect a written description of the process that a software innovator wishes to protect. For the sake of copyright law, the program which directs the computer to perform the process is treated as a manuscript that describes what is to be done. This computer-language description is then protected, and no computer may have that description read into it without permission of the copyright holder. Since copyright standards require that no copyright may be used to limit access to the procedures that are described in the copyrighted material, there must in theory be some alternative, unprotected statement of the rules which may be used to direct the machine to perform the same processes. So copyright protections are under some circumstances also inadequate protection for computer innovation.

The situation as it now stands is that computer researches perceive an injustice in the unauthorized reproduction of innovative programming techniques, but have inadequate legal recourse to prevent it. With slight exaggeration, we may characterize the present situation as one that leaves a whole class of design innovations without any relevant legal notion of property, even though professionals may intuitively see them as "belonging" to their designers. On this view, there are areas of concern for computer professionals that lie outside of any legal consideration. It may then seem that an association of computer professionals may move to establish standards for themselves without any conflict with established law. To the contrary, I argue that no association should attempt to fill the legal vacuum, even with a code that applies only to the members of the association itself.

In the long run, we must revise the standards for property rights over innovation so that those perceived injustices will be legally recognized. In the short run, however we may seek some stopgap solution. The technology itself may be modified to ease the difficulty. We may for instance make it difficult to pirate software by incorporating programs into physically impenetrable firmware or by boobytrapping programs against unauthorized users. Also the courts may attempt to distort the traditional legal categories to cover the new situation, as in my opinion the Court did in <u>Diehr</u>. Contrary to the common conception of lawyers as the champions of sneaky sophistic argument, however, these "solutions" that depend on fine legal points are generally frowned on by the courts. At issue in this paper is how professional societies can react to these legally unrecognized injustices in the practice of the new technology. In the particular case of protection for software, can the major associations for computer professionals (such as the Association for Computer Machinery, and the Institute for Electrial and Electric Engineers) propose new standards for design independence to their membership? Although I see nothing wrong with publicizing a proposition for new standards, I argue that no association should act to institute the practice of those standards among its members.

As we should expect, the problem of applying traditional standards for the protection of innovative design to new technologies is not unique to the computer industry. Very similar problems have in this century confronted, for instance, the motion picture industry and the fashion design industry. And in latter case, a private fashion designer's associations did step in to establish a standard for respect of design innovation. The history of that failure is exemplary of what is wrong with privately established standards.

Until the 2nd half of the 19th century, most clothing was hand made. But in this century, new technology has made it possible for general distributors to provide even high quality clothing. In this industrial environment there is a new issue of intellectual property rights for clothing designs. Designers (such as Calvin Klein, Christian Dior, Coco Chanel, Yves Saint-Laurent) find that their work is simply copied by other distributors who need not face design costs or who do not have the skill for independent design. Except for trademark, there is little protection. There is practially no legal recourse when a cheaper outlet provides jeans just like designer jeans except for the pocket design.

We should note how closely the clothing design problem resembles the software problem. Both issues arose when new technology placed emphasis on design innovations which are not recognized as intellectual property under the law. Moreover the reasons that clothing designs are inadequately protected by either patent or copyright are nearly the same as the reasons software is unprotected. The designs do not describe machines or processes such as are protected by patent, and copyrights on the designs do not provide protection for clothing based on the ideas expressed in those designs. It may indeed be harder for fashion designers than for software designers to protect their work, since some trade secret protection may be available for software that is only narrowly distributed. What is called "software piracy" in one industry is called "design piracy" in the other.

In the 1930's, the Fashion Guild of America attempted to impose a standard for independence of design upon itself. As far as I can tell, the standard was carefully and fairly enforced. Designs were registered with the Guild. Disputes were heard before an unbiased tribunal with provisions for appeal. Violations lead to expulsion from the Guild, and it was deemed a further violation to trade with censored organizations. In 1941, the Supreme Court finally decided that the Guild's actions were illegal.[4]

The narrow basis for the cease and desist order was antitrust law. The Court noted that the Guild was attempting to monopolize the fashion industry through the establishment of a tough standard and the boycott of noncomplying firms. I am, however, not particularly interested in anti-trust law per se, or in the notion of open commerce defined by it. The wider issue is the enforcement of standards by private associations lacking any apparent authority to establish or enforce standards. Justice Black's majority opinion notes that:

> In addition to all this, the combination is in reality an extra-governmental agency, which prescribes rules for the regulation and restraint of interstate commerce, and pro-

vides extra-judicial tribunals for determination and punishment of violations, and 'trenches upon the power of the national legislature and violates the statute'.[5]

The point is that certain bodies have the authority to establish standards and that the private association is not such a body. I am more concerned for the encroachments "upon the power of the national legislature" than with the violation of the statute. I now attempt to provide the argument that justifies prohibition of association action, even in situations when association standards fit into a vacuum in current law and thus conflict with no current law.

#2. Rights to Set Private Standards

In part my argument forbidding private associations to set standards is simply the rebuttal of an argument that would permit them to independently set standards. I argue for judicial review by refuting arguments that purport to show that associations have a right to set standards without review. The argument is far from conclusive. It does oversimplify the complex matter of legal jurisdiction in the U.S. system. It also leaves open the possibility that, through judicial review, the courts may decide to let associations set standards as a matter of policy. Then, even though review is possible, it would seem reasonable to say that a limited authority to set standards has been acquired by private associations. Still, I think the argument has merit. So I initially argue simply against any right of associations to set standards. The additional matters will be taken up in #3.

There is a common, and I believe particularly naive, view of private associations as independent self-governing bodies that may establish their own membership policies, no matter how crazy. The argument says that since I may associate with whom I wish, I may constitute a private association along any lines I wish. I may form an association for the play of softball with four outs per inning, or the encouragement of design independence in the fashion industry. Indeed freedom to associate or to form an association almost seems like a basic human right. It may be simply an oversight that it was not mentioned in the U.S. Constitution along with freedom of assembly and free speech. The Court has in fact said in recent cases that there is a right to associate inherent in the Constitution, suggested by or included within the "penumbra" of rights listed in the Bill of Rights and warranting the same protection. Since I may associate as I wish, it seems I may constitute an association as I wish with membership restricted as I wish, even to the point of silliness. I may exclude, it seems, professional athletes, style pirates, and those who keep aspidistras. On this view what I call an invalid assumption of the power to set standards is really nothing more than the exercise of a right to associate with only those who respect the rights of software innovators. The courts have occasionally taken this hands-off attitude towards membership policies.[6]

Even the most radical proponents of the hands-off view of private associations admit qualifications. It is generally acknowledged that the state acquires a right to oversee membership policies when it grants special tax breaks or state licenses. Also few would object to state interference if the association membership violates particular statutes.

Those who wish to maintain a right of associations to set standards unaffected by anti-trust will attempt to distinguish two claims. The stronger claim is that the state has authority to review any standards the members of a private association may set for themselves. The weaker says that the state may interfere with the self-imposition of standards when those standards restrict the conduct of non-members on matters which are a recognized state interest. The stronger thesis entails the weaker. The weaker thesis recognizes the authority of the state under anti-trust law to limit self-imposed standards that affect trade since open trade has in prior analysis been shown a proper state interest. The stronger, in the extreme, grants state authority to review dress codes of private clubs, etc.

I argue for the stronger thesis. In practice, that means that I would remove the burden from the state to justify jurisdiction in a challenge of association rules. This is contrary to current practice whereby the courts will not enter into a dispute without first establishing, for instance, that the standards influence business practice and thus may be challenged within the context of anti-trust law. The attitude the weaker thesis is nicely reflected in the views of a one-time member of the justice department that the standards of a small association might not be challenged if the association has only slight influence on business practice: "...the greater the business advantage in an association, the less control the association may exercise over its membership."[7]

It will be argued against me that I confuse the stronger and weaker theses, and attempt to justify the stronger with arguments that only justify the weaker. Thus the argument for a hands off view of private standards is only "naive" if it is used to refute the weaker thesis, but stands against my stronger claim.

The hands off argument works, in so far as it does, by appealing to an intuition that a state oversteps its natural authority when it interferes with personal, or entirely self-regarding, acts. It attempts to establish that the self-imposition of standards by an association is a private self-regarding act of the association. The notion of a self-regarding act has often been shown to be vague and of dubious value as a basis for legal doctrine. And any argument that depends so centrally on that notion is on weak footing from the start. At best the notion provides a rough and ready sense of personal rights. (The courts have used a similar rough and ready sense of a right to self-determination in personal or simply "private" matters to decide on such diverse issues as methods of birth control and the termination of life support systems. But it has wisely refused to make the notion precise.) Although I accept some such notion as a principle with regard to personal action, I do not accept the application to private associations.

It may seem that if each member of an association of computer professionals joins in the establishment of a standard for independence of software design, then the standard is just the combined statement of each member's self-regarding right to live by a standard of respect for software innovation. On this view, the enforcement of the standard by an association upon its own membership imposes the authority of the association on one of those persons whose right to accept the standards is the basis of the association's right to establish the standards. I grant that in some circumstances an act of censorship may be a self-regarding act of the censored member. I may accept rules even when I fall afoul of them. But I do not see how we can maintain this view of an association's authority to set standards if there is a dispute over standards, particularly if the dispute is so serious that a member may wish judicial review of the standards.

If a dispute over standards breaks out which is serious enough to warrant appeal to the courts, the standard cannot be viewed as the member's own personal standard. Therefore in this case, we must reject the ideal picture of a professional association consisting of individuals choosing to live by a self-imposed standard. If each association member personally accepts the standard, then there is never need to appeal the association's authority. I have no objection to an association that wishes to state universally accepted commonplaces. But there is no need for an appeal procedure on such rules, for there would never be a dispute over them. A standard whose validity is never questioned does not need an association's authority to back it up. The interesting cases always center about an appeal to the association to enforce its standards or to revise them. That is, it always centers on disagreements over standards. So in each interesting case, the association does not act as a body of individuals who are excercising a right to associate with others with similar standards.

#3. Significant Standards and Legal Codes

A standard for design independence might be adopted by a private association without any measures for its enforcement. I see little wrong with a standard that is merely a policy statement for an association or a model for a legal code of design independence. It may be argued, in fact, that associations have a right to propose and publish standards as a matter of free speech.[8] And it certainly is a right of associations to petition the government to set standards.[9] I believe, in fact, that my prescription against enforced standards is a ground for permitting associations broad powers to forcefully publicize proposed standards. Professionals should certainly have some means to influence their professional standards. If we do not permit them to enforce standards, they must have other means to influence them.

The central issue is whether the association can expect its membership to live by its code. If the association merely presents a standard with no guard against violation, then the association may hope for, but cannot seriously expect, compliance in a fiercely competitive market. Universal compliance may in itself indicate that a published code has acquired the status of a strict rule, even if there are no obvious enforcement procedures.[10] At question is whether associations should act with authority to enforce a standard for design independence. The A.C.M. has both a code of ethics and a carefully detailed procedure for investigating possible violations and for censoring violators. If it were to risk the wrath of the justice department by writing a standard for design independence into its code, the standard would be enforced by a complex legalistic procedure leading to possible expulsion from the association.

There is a wide range of methods that have been adopted by associations to enforce their codes. Everyone will agree that associations have no authority to impose the extreme sorts of punishments (e.g. incarceration) that may be imposed by the state. On the other extreme, few would object to a program that simply publicized the standards and made no attempt to censor violations. In between there are a myriad of alternatives: the bar associations of several states send letters of reprimand, the commissioner of baseball imposes fines. It is a common misconception that the "milder" forms of reprimand are trivial and may be assumed by associations without philosophical scrutiny of its assumed authority. But no forms of reprimand are trivial. A letter from the bar association hurts professional standing. Even exclusion from a social club often means a great deal more to a member who depends on that club's social life than the fines that a criminal court may impose. It is, I believe, a failing of our legal system that it does not adequately protect members from the harm done them by private associations even when that harm cannot be measured in terms of traditional harms of monetary loss, etc. Zecharia Chafee has argued that the courts should recognize and protect a "member's relation to the association" as a thing of value to the member in itself.[11] Following Chafee, I seek no further for a basis for court jurisdiction.

When an association adopts an enforcement procedure for its code, it takes on a similar role to the state court system. This is not a trivial move. Hobbes has pointed out that, in the case of civil society in general, the individual who gives an association this role, foregoes certain rights that he otherwise holds as an independent moral agent. Unless he gives up the right to decide for himself what he ought to do in a given situation, the constitution of the association is meaningless. That is, if the association's code merely reflects the unanimous choice of each member or if the association grants to each member the freedom to obey or disobey a code, then the association is not a civil body. And when the individual joins an association with the power to enact and enforce a code (even with trivial reprimands), he no longer decides for himself how to act. This is an immediate consequence of the definition of membership in an association with an enforced code. It is a misnomer for the A.C.M. to call its code a "code of ethics" when its enforcement procedure turns that code into a legal document in competition with state law. This point has been eloquently argued by John Ladd.[12]

Hobbes argues further that since a citizen of state generally foregoes the right to independent decision for the sake of the civil state, he cannot further pass that right to a private association without the explicit permission of the state. Thus Hobbes argues that a private association that attempts to set a standard for design independence in the absence of a civil law governing this sort of intellectual property would detract from the authority of the state, and confuse the notion of property.[13] Hobbes grants to the state alone the ability to set standards (or delegate that ability) in matters such as design standards that bear on intellectual property.

Hobbes' targets are the trade guilds--exactly the sorts of association at question in this paper. His attitude is reflected in the present government distrust of private associations and the fervent anti-trust challenge to them. The opposing attitude is the guild attitude that restricts trade to members of private associations acting outside of and often against state interest. On this I agree with Hobbes. Standards for design independence are exactly the sort of thing that is properly set by the state or its agents.

Hobbes' argument turns on a demand for a unified civil authority. He cannot imagine a state that functions smoothly when codes on different practices are established by independent bodies. But we may note today many governments (including the U.S.) that do function smoothly with widely dispersed and fairly independent governing bodies. We could even consider the federal government as one legalistic association among many which we have joined and to which we acknowledge a right to set standards (although, as Chafee points out, one with exceptionally high annual dues). Then so long as we do not fool ourselves by confusing decisions based on an association code with a personal ethical decision, we may countenance private associations that expect their members to live by the associations' standards. On this view, associations get the authority to enforce rules in the same way (however it is analyzed) as the larger association which is the state.

We may, indeed, be more likely to trust a representative of a professional society to give a reasonable and sensitive ruling on an issue of software privacy than to trust a federal judge who poorly understands the technology. My personal bias is, however, to accept established court authority in these matters and generally to grant the authority to establish rules to as few additional associations as possible. I, of course, note that the courts often authorize associations to act on their behalf. Many states have "integrated" bar associations. That is, one association acts both as a private association for lawyers and as a public body representing the state in matters of legal ethics. But then the authority flows from the state to the association over which it maintains control. The association is no longer simply private. That is the Hobbesian view that I espouse here.

My argument at this point may seem weak: I generally opt for the Hobbesian view without conclusive argument. But the Hobbesian view has greater force in the particular case of rules against software piracy. At issue here is the definition of property. Standards for design independence act to create a notion of personal property over designs. It contributes to the notion of property that is generally defined in the laws of theft, transfer, patent, trespass, inheritance, etc., all of which are defined in state code or common law with state authority. A private standard in this area clearly intrudes on state authority.

We distinguished in #2 between a strong claim that the state always has authority over the standards of private associations and a weak claim that the state has authority over standards that touch on matters of state interest. I claimed then that I was going to argue for the stronger, more controversial claim. It may appear that I am now falling back on the weaker claim, looking at property as an area of established state interest. But we are not simply backsliding to the philosophically uninteresting weaker thesis of #2. Contrary to the weak thesis, I argue here against any private code for design independence regardless of the effect that a code may have on non-association members. Also contrary to my views, the weaker thesis would permit private associations to impose software standards upon themselves if we accept the above characterization of the present legal picture as leaving a vacuum in the area of software design. I argue that standards of design independence are included in the broad area of intellectual property which is wholly a matter for state determination. I do not believe that we must establish a particular state interest in design independence. State authority is established by the fact that the state generally acts to define the notion of property, which is inherent in the laws of theft, inheritance, etc. Thus I argue that the whole question of property is a matter of primary state responsibility, even though the state has left the question of design property entirely undetermined.

The present discussion may suggest a distinction similar to the distinction of #2 between the weak and strong claim, but this is a different distinction and should not be confused with the earlier one. I do maintain the strong thesis that all association rules may be appealed to state authority. But the present discussion suggests that the possibility of appeal is an insufficient check of private standards in some situations. Even if we reject Hobbes' demand for a unified civil authority in all matters, we must recognize its primary responsibility in the creation of the notion of property. This is an area where the possibility of appeal to the civil court is an insufficient check on the authority of the association over its rules. Thus we may generally distinguish two sorts of association rules. An association may assume the authority to establish reasonable membership dues without prior authorization. Although dues levels should on my view be open to judicial review, they should (except in very odd cases) be upheld as a matter of course. But associations may not step in with standards on matters such as property which are significantly determined by the state, even in questions of intellectual property created by new technology unanticipated by the state.

My views suggest greater government intrusion into the affairs of private associations than is now admitted. I am not pleased with that result. Among other things, this may tend to impart to associations a rigidity that could destroy many of the advantages association practice has over government activity. But that rigidity is a natural consequence of any attempt by an association to accept the role of a setter of standards. Even prior to judicial review, we can see that rigidity set in when an association such as the A.C.M. adopts a legalistic document like its present procedures for the enforcement of its "code of ethics." If an association does not wish to be viewed as a governing body within the governmental structure, it simply must avoid doing those things that governmental bodies do.

Illinois Institute of Technology

NOTES

1. Michael Davis, Professor of Philosophy at Illinois State University, wrote a lengthy criticism of an early version of the present paper. The paper as it now stands incorporates several of his suggestions.

2. *Diamond v. Diehr,* 101 S.Ct. 1048 (1981). I more or less agree with Justice Stevens' position in the dissent.

3. *Apple Computer, Inc. v. Franklin Computer Corporation,* 3rd Circuit Court of Appeals, No. 82-1582.

4. *Fashion Originators Guild of America v. Federal Trade Commission,* 61 S.Ct. 703.

5. *Ibid.* p. 707.

6. See *North Dakota v. North Central Association of Colleges,* 33 F. Supp. 649, 1938.

7. John Bodner, quoted in George Webster, *Law of Associations,* pp. 2-53.

8. See Phillip Kissam, "Antitrust Law, The First Amendment, and Professional Self-Regulation of Technical Quality," in R. Blair and S. Rubin, *Regulating the Professions.*

9. See *Eastern Railroad Presidents Conference v. Noerr Motor Freight* 365 U.S. 127 (1961).

10. See *Goldfarb v. Virginia State Bar* 421 U.S. 773.

11. Zecharia Chafee, "The International Affairs of Associations Not for Profit," *Harvard Law Review,* May 1930.

12. John Ladd, "The Quest for a Code of Professional Ethics," in R. Chalk, M. Frankel, & S. Chafer, *AAAS Professional Ethics Project.*

13. See e.g. *The Citizen,* V. 10.

ON WHAT OUGHT WE VOTE?
ON PROFESSIONAL ORGANIZATIONS AND PUBLIC AFFAIRS

Robert Strikwerda

1. What issues are appropriate for consideration by a voluntary professional association such as the American Philosophical Association (APA) or the Ohio Philosophical Association (OPA)? Consider the following two items, both approved at the Annual Meeting of the Western Division of the APA, April 27, 1984, for submission to its membership for a vote by mail ballot:
> Be it resolved that the APA Western Division declares its unqualified opposition to any United States support for military attacks on Nicaragua and the use of United States funds and/or personnel in such attacks....
>> (1) Believing that the First Amendment requires the freest possible exchange of ideas, we oppose any restrictions on
>> -- the import of ideas and information into the U.S.;
>> -- visits by any person to the U.S. because of that person's beliefs or lawful political activity or association;
>> -- travel abroad by Americans because of their political beliefs, activities, or associations; and
>> -- export of ideas or information which may be lawfully circulated in the U.S.
>> (2) We approve APA's joining the ad hoc coalition designed to eliminate restriction on the free movement of individuals, information, and ideas across the American border....[1]

Or the following, passed by the Eastern Division in 1982:
> Resolved: We, the members of the APA, Eastern Division, regard as an improper exercise of congressional power the passage of any and all legislation which would specify when human life begins.[2]

Two letters from philosophers protesting the impropriety of the measure were printed in a later issue of the APA Proceedings.[3]

Should such resolutions be considered by professional associations? Are some appropriate and others inappropriate? Can any guidelines delimiting the proper scope of consideration be provided? Does a member who dissents on some issue have moral grounds for complaint, grounds I call those of unjustified compromising involvement? In this paper I argue that, given the nature of professional associations, compromising involvement of the minority is sufficient grounds to preclude consideration of resolutions concerning issues that fall outside the primary purposes of the association, unless certain specific conditions are present to override this factor of compromising involvement.

2. In dealing with normative issues philosophers have concentrated on two types of actors: individuals and governments. While these are undoubtedly the most important, there is a vast range of "intermediate" actors: universities, businesses, unions, computer user groups, etc. I see professional associations as a subset of the set of voluntary organized associations. By organized associations I intend those groups with constitutions or the like, in which the members take positions and undertake activities in some explicit fashion such as voting. These include neighborhood block organizations, but not neighborhoods, the APA, but not the philosophic profession in the U.S. Although my examples come from the APA, the issues have a broader significance, not simply for other professional organizations, but also for any organized association. My focus here is also only on one activity, passing resolutions on public policy issues without further actions by the association, such as making financial contributions.

3. Professional associations are typically thought of as voluntary; employment in a philosophy department is not contingent upon membership in the APA. Those who do not join regional associations such as the OPA probably simply lose the opportunity to enjoy the interchange of ideas and ensuing discussion and conviviality. The primary purpose of the association is to provide and promote these; the reasons people join are to obtain these goods, which are "intrinsic" to the activities of the association. Participation does not provide benefits for the member in terms of effects on other organi-

zations or other activities: "extrinsic" factors. There are constraining factors in the case of the APA: graduate students seeking academic employment would be hindered if they could not utilize the APA interviewing facilities, career advancement might be hindered if one did not come to the conventions, meet fellow philosophers, deliver papers, and the like. Some may rise to prominence and financial success--such as it is--in philosophy without participation in the APA, American Catholic Philosophical Association, or the Philosophy of Science Association, but I think it unusual. Here the retort, "If you don't like it, leave it.", has a limited plausibility, though more than in the case of nation-states.

The centrality of these intrinsic goods, such as intellectual interchange, resulting from participation in the activities of professional associations distinguishes them from other organizations such as block clubs or unions, typically formed in large part with reference to other organizations, an extrinsic goal. Further, professional associations are the major arena for such activities; witness the tendency for smaller, special interest philosophic societies to meet in conjunction with the APA divisional conventions. They are not quite monopolies, but they do seem to dominate the market. Although many philosophers do not participate in professional associations, for many participation in the APA is inseparable from much of their professional activity.

Given the nature of such associations, does a member have moral grounds for protesting that it is illegitimate for the association to pass resolutions on various issues? Passage of resolutions such as those listed above are neither significant reasons for joining nor central to the primary purposes of the association. Are they thereby inappropriate?

4. There are two ideal types that can serve as foils; the first I call the "unrestricted" association. In its defense one might argue that a voluntary organization may take positions on whatever issues it pleases as long as it stays within the law. Whatever the majority decides to consider is appropriate. Here we might have a close to pure case of majority makes right, perhaps limited by procedural constraints such as giving opposing speakers reasonable opportunity to speak. There could be pragmatic objections to consideration. Debates could be time consuming, embitter some, or cause some to resign mem-

bership. But if these do not occur to an appreciable extent then no grounds--given this ideal type--exist for questioning the propriety of such votes.

5. In the other ideal type, which I term the "restricted" association, the boundaries of acceptable resolutions are defined very narrowly, whether done explicitly in the charter or not. Only those matters touching on the primary purpose of the organization, in this case, the internal benefits to the members, are appropriate. The purpose of the OPA or APA might be defined solely as the sharing of philosophical ideas via personal interaction through the reading and critique of philosophical papers, and only those matters directly pertaining to this would be considered.

But there are factors which weigh against such a policy. Issues may arise which cry out for a broader scope or focus. Governmental actions might affect philosophers quite directly: perhaps a way of drawing the boundaries between the NSF and NEH or a state ruling on college requirements, such as requiring a critical thinking course as was done recently in California. Colleagues may be hindered in their professional or pedagogic activities as the result of racial or sex discrimination. Issues with a substantial philosophic component can become central in national political debate, for example ones concerning the relevance of scientific evidence to ethical questions such as the morality of abortion or the status of creationism as a scientific theory.

There seem to be at least three grounds to justify an association's involvement: there is either substantial impact on the members in their professional life or a moral responsibility to speak out on matters affecting colleagues or a social responsibility to exercise some relevant expertise, either directly philosophical or resulting from being educators, as most philosophers are at present. Given the potentially encompassing scope of philosophy, I believe this expertise should be construed conservatively.

These grounds are not necessarily sufficient justification. Those member-philosophers who are interested in such matters could form a new "Philosophers for Action" organization, similar to PANDORA, "Philosophers Against Nuclear Destruction of Rational Animals," now Concerned Philosophers. And their philosophic opponents could form another. Such specific organizations, and involvement of philosophers in them, would constitute the best response to those who might indict the APA and philosophers of the "crime of silence." The silence of an organization would not indict it or the members of that organization if they participate in other organizations which do take a position and work to bring about a specific outcome. (This is a sufficient and perhaps a necessary condition.) These could be continuing organizations of generally like-minded professionals, who would accept occasional disagreement with the majority as a necessary concomitant of the benefits of a more politically active policy. The reasons for involvement in it are extrinsic, not intrinsic.

Yet there are problems with such a practice in some cases: slowness of reaction if no activist group of professionals is already organized and the expectation of governments that the official professional organizations respond for the profession. If professional organizations of other disciplines, such as the American Historical Society or American Astronomical Association, involve themselves in some fashion, the failure of the APA to follow suit may render the actions of philosophers much less effective. Further, action by the APA seems appropriate in cases affecting philosophical colleagues in other countries. Adverse treatment of colleagues, whether or not actually members of the organization, challenges the purpose of the organization and its discipline. It is also likely, one, that professional contacts would be among the first outside of a country to learn of a professional's oppression or imprisonment, and two, that a protest from the APA might have more effect then an ad hoc group of philosophers or perhaps even an organization expressly formed to protest and alleviate such conditions, for example, an Academics Amnesty International. These could provide moral grounds for overriding the objections of those members who do not wish to take such actions.

6. In many situations the pragmatic considerations against an unrestricted policy would not be compelling. The question turns, instead, on the assessment of the extent to which a member opposing a resolution is morally involved by the association taking the contrary position. Is there such involvement, does it constitute a compromise of the minority and how serious is this compromise? I do not know of any entirely satisfactory way to address these issues. One starting point

is one of the letters of protest mentioned above, in which the nine signers described their reaction to the resolution on the propriety of Congressional action on the beginning of life as follows:

> ...we are sensitive to the plight of those members who find the APA adopting a resolution, at least the spirit of which flouts their deepest moral and religious convictions--and in some cases the teachings of the churches with which their educational institutions are affiliated....Yet we find it hard to believe that all who voted in favor of the resolution in question deliberately sought to compromise their colleagues and friends.[4]

While not sharing these particular convictions, I find it hard to gainsay such a claim of having been compromised. Underlying such a protest is a conception of a professional association as--however attenuated--a moral community. When it takes a position, however rancorous and divided the prior debate, the position it takes is sent to the government and general public as the position of the association.[5] As such, all members do have some involvement. Resignations in protest take their moral significance from this fact. Where the positions an association adopts relate to moral and political issues those in the minority can justifiably claim that they have experienced some moral compromise through their membership. That they continue to participate in the discussion, etc., while gritting their teeth does not obviate the difficulty. Indeed the minority could be said to have a prima facie right not to be so compromised. I prefer to say that the majority has a duty to provide an acceptable reason to override the minority protest in such instances. I do not take this right of the minority to be particularly strong; I think there are frequently good reasons for the APA to speak out.. It does have a responsibility to articulate these reasons.

Some such compromise is inevitable due to membership in an association. For instance, if the majority of the OPA elects an advocate of very restrictive abortion laws as president, those in the association opposed to such a policy may have to tolerate some difficulties as a consequence. Friends and colleagues in other disciplines might question the choice and see it as indicative of some deeper philosophic tendency. Some members of the Division might earnestly wish to be disassociated from the choice, even if no one outside the association takes note, but given that a majority wish this philosopher as their leader, that it was done in the proper fashion, etc., this sort of involvement is inevitable. However, voting. for or against a proposition on U.S. involvement in Nicaragua is not equally unavoidable.

7. What guidelines do I propose?
Vote on only those issues:
1. which affect members in their capacity as professionals or in the carrying out of their professional activities, OR
2. where a majority of the members of the professional organization have some specific expertise or knowledge, AND
3. where no effective specific focused organization is present or feasible, given, for instance, constraints of time, OR
4. there is strong expectation on the part of other organizations that the organization respond to the issue and great utility to be gained if it does so, given this expectation.

In more perspicuous form (1 or [2 and (3 or 4)]).

Some comments: These guidelines would allow protest of restrictions on philosophers and other academics in either other countries or our own. I do not think some immediate connection of philosophic activity and the restriction is necessary to justify a protest. They would allow the proposed resolution on the free movement of ideas but not the protest of U.S. actions in Central America. Given the present situation in the U.S. where governmental grants, etc. are allocated in part through advice from the various professional organizations, resolutions on these matters would be appropriate.

8. There is one justification specific to voting on nuclear war questions that deserves mention: that the magnitude of this issue justifies balloting in this case, while consideration of other issues even though of great moral seriousness would be inappropriate. A problem with this justification, at least as I have heard it used, is the unjustified assumption that the greater magnitude of the issue justifies overriding other moral considerations in this

context. Further, granting it this overriding force questions the very participation of the proponents in the APA or OPA. The very involvement of most supporters in APA activities shows that they do not take it to override their own ordinary concerns. Here I submit that the burden of proof must lie on the advocates of consideration of such a measure. They must show that there is some close connection between the actions of the professional organization and the event to be averted or brought about such that there is no other alternative organization, e.g. PANDORA or another citizen group, that can substitute.

9. A related matter is the manner in which the professional organization addresses such issues. Resolutions likely presuppose various substantive principles which a philosophic association with a clear conscience would want to discuss before endorsing. Further, philosophical discussion of the issues might contribute to public discussion. In any event, to take a position which may affront deeply held beliefs or one's colleagues without discussion and clarification, allowing them to voice their arguments, is questionable for any professional organization, much less the APA. It should also strive for impartiality, e.g. addressing problems for colleagues in South Africa as well as Poland, perhaps praising as well as condemning.

10. Even though the APA might not take an explicit stand on an issue, it need not avoid the issue. The APA could facilitate organization of specifically focused associations of scholars, perhaps through furnishing mailing lists or allowing members to contribute an extra amount in their dues which the APA would channel to the organization. It could also undertake or at least encourage educational activities which would address the issues. It could appoint commissions to study the issues; perhaps these--but not the APA itself--could be allowed to make recommendations. Sponsoring such activities may also raise questions of morally compromising involvement, but here the responsibility of a professional organization to involve itself in public issues outweighs this concern.

11. There are many questions presently considered proper matters for organizational consideration that the

above guidelines would preclude. It would be an error to see this as giving a conservative cast to my analysis. Social activism does not necessarily require the diversion of organizations from their present activities; it may require the creation of new ones.[6]

University of Wisconsin at La Crosse

NOTES

1. *Proceedings and Addresses of the American Philosophical Association*, Vol. 57, No. 4, March 1984, p. 502.

2. *Proceedings and Addresses of the American Philosophical Association*, Vol. 56, No. 1, Sept. 1982, p. 92.

3. *Proceedings and Addresses of the American Philosophical Association*, Vol. 56, No. 3, Feb. 1983, pp. 443-444.

4. *Ibid,* see note 3.

5. Some proponents of consideration of a public policy issue tacitly recognize this community by arguing that the APA has a moral responsibility to address an issue. I am arguing that it must also recognize an additional, competing responsibility.

6. This paper has benefitted from comments by David Hoekema, Edward Langerak, Donald Scherer, Penny Weiss and the many participants in the discussion at the Bowling Green Conference.